The Vegetarian Diet For Kidney Disease Treatment

Preserving Kidney Function With Plant Based Eating

by

Joan Brookhyser, RD, CD, CSR

First published by AuthorHouse 09/17/04

ISBN: 1-4184-6031-1 (e-book)
ISBN: 1-4184-3287-3 (Paperback)

This book is printed on acid free paper.

ACKNOWLEDGEMENTS

The following people were instrumental in the development and publication of this book:

Carol Kinzner, RN, ARNP, Kathy Harvey, MS,RD, Kerri Wiggins, MS,RD, Maude Valentine, RN, Anne Mesaros, RD,CDE; Judy Clark and Amy Putnum.

I also want to thank the many patients I have worked with over the years who have given me the motivation to write this book.

And finally I want to thank my life partner and best friend Pat Hogan who provided ongoing encouragement and support of my dream; to have this book published, to make a difference in the lives of those people who are coping with chronic kidney disease.

To my Life Partner, Pat

And

My daughter, Danielle

Table of Contents

INTRODUCTION

VEGETARIANISM IN KIDNEY DISEASE

When I first became a dietitian over 20 years ago, vegetarianism and kidney disease did not mix. If you were a vegetarian you were advised to let go of your herbivore ways. If you were curious about becoming a vegetarian you were discouraged. The research at that time saw plant proteins as inferior to animal proteins. This inferiority was thought to cause people with kidney disease to become sicker or more uremic from their condition. In addition, it was thought that plant proteins were too high in many of the minerals that needed to be restricted in kidney disease, thus causing more complications. However, in the last decade further research has changed this viewpoint and we now know this not to be the case.

Vegan, lacto-ovo vegetarian or occasional vegetarian eating can fit with your kidney disease. Vegetarianism is not only acceptable, it is being found to be superior to animal based diets in kidney disease prevention and treatment. By following the guidelines in this book you can continue or begin a plant based diet to help, not hinder, your kidney health.

The information provided is not only intended to promote a healthy plant based diet, but to help you in planning the healthiest diet possible for long term health and fitness. In the years I have worked with people having kidney disease, I have seen them not die from their kidney disease but other conditions such as heart disease, infections, diabetes complications or cancer. A well-planned diet is at the forefront of this battle of health before you and helps reduce your risk of complications. A well-planned diet is not only necessary for plant based eating but healthy eating in general.

This book is not meant to replace your medical care. Kidney disease treatment works best with routine visits to your physician and following your medical treatment recommendations, in addition to good nutritional management.

This book has been designed to help those with greater than 30% kidney function not receiving dialysis treatment, and those receiving dialysis treatment and less than 15 % kidney function. If you are experiencing kidney disease with less than 30% kidney function, professional assistance is strongly recommended. This would include seeking the individualized counseling of a dietitian who is certified in the specialty of renal nutrition.

Such dietitians can be found by contacting:

The National Kidney Foundation 1-800-622-9010

The American Dietetic Association 1-800-877-1600

TERMINOLOGY:

Even though I have attempted to minimize unnecessary medical jargon, many of these words are needed to help in the understanding and self treatment of your disease. The Appendix contains a glossary of these words.

A NOTE TO THE PROFESSIONAL:

This book is not meant to replace professional nutritional management or health care. However, I often find patients desiring to seek resources outside the "traditional" health care arena and, as a result, receiving dangerous or harmful advice. In an effort to combat potential misinformation, I have wanted to make valid information available to the people who seek it. It is my hope as a health care professional that you can utilize the information in this book in the care of your patients who desire a vegetarian lifestyle.

Chapter One
Benefits of Vegetarianism

BENEFITS OF VEGETARIANISM

The benefit of vegetarianism in kidney disease begins with prevention of the disease itself. Vegetarianism is one of many lifestyle components that can help in preventing complications that lead to a decline in kidney function. High blood pressure places more pressure on the vascular system of the kidney and can cause kidney damage. High lipid levels in the blood can lead to blood vessel narrowing, heart disease, and kidney problems. Plant-based eating is low in fat and high in the nutrients that prevent these diseases, or delay their complications, leading the way to preserving the health of your kidneys.

If you have just found out that you have kidney disease, a plant-based diet can slow down it's progression and possibly help with other problems associated with that disease. Research suggests that the amino acids that make up plant-based proteins may be less stressful on the kidneys, than animal based proteins, which in turn may slow down the rate of kidney damage. This slowing of the damage happens by decreasing pressure on the glomeruli, or filters, of the kidney. This can help control blood pressure and decrease proteinuria, or protein in the urine. Protein loss in the urine is a sign of progressive kidney damage. The more protein loss, the more kidneys damage. If you are diabetic a vegetarian diet, properly planned with consistent carbohydrates, will help improve diabetic control. Improved diabetic control also lessens the progression of kidney loss and function.

If you have kidney disease, and require dialysis, a vegetarian diet can also be of benefit to you. Cardiac disease is the number one reason for death in dialysis patients; a vegetarian diet can help decrease harmful fats or lipids in the blood, and decrease this health risk. In addition, a plant-based diet can lower homocysteine levels in the blood. Homocysteine levels, a precursor to heart disease, have been found to be higher in kidney disease.

Plants, not animals, are the source of phytochemicals. The added benefits and functions of phytochemicals (also known as: saponins, indoles, allyl sulfides, ellagic acid, isoflavnes, phenolic acids) are just beginning to surface. What we know is that these nutrients are potent antioxidants. Kidney diseases such as glomerulernephritis may be benefited by a diet high in antioxidants. In addition for people with kidney disease, as with people without kidney disease, a strong immune system is important. A diet high in these nutrients can help your immune system remain strong, preventing other diseases, infections or possible cancers.

Fiber becomes important. People with kidney disease need to have a diet high in other disease fighting components. Foods high in fiber, and phytochemicals, are the best defense for this need. In planning a diet that is plentiful in plants, and minimal in processed foods and animal proteins, you can be well on your way to living a healthy life even with kidney disease.

MYTHS OF VEGETARIANISM IN KIDNEY DISEASE

There are many myths that surround vegetarianism in kidney disease. These myths are based on the assumption that plant proteins are incomplete, unbalanced or even dangerous in kidney disease. This is no truer of plant based diets than of a animal-based diet. The three myths that follow are the most common you will hear.

Myth #1: Vegetarian diets do not provide quality protein

Quality protein no longer equals animal protein. Historically, animal proteins were thought to be the only good quality protein to obtain all of your amino acids perfectly balanced without the concern of excess nitrogen wastes.

Early in the 20th century, protein quality was assessed on the basis of a particular protein to support the growth of rapidly growing baby rats. This technique was called PER (Protein Efficiency Ratio). These studies indicated that eggs and other animal products had a higher biological value of protein than plant products, or in other words, made healthier rats. As a result, this led to the assumption that humans also needed these same proteins. This theory is now history, for we are not rats! The growth and therefore protein needs of rats are different from that of humans.

In 1989 the International Food and Agriculture Organization (FAO), the World Health Organization (WHO) and the United States Department of Agriculture (USDA) adopted the Protein Digestibility-Corrected Amino Acid Score (PDCAAS) as the official assay for evaluation of protein quality. The PDDCAS takes into account a protein's essential amino acid composition, corrected for digestibility and referenced to the two-to-five year old human requirement pattern. This new method of evaluating protein quality found that plant proteins provide high quality protein.

Several studies have looked at the impact of animal and plant protein on the function of healthy kidneys. When protein amount was equivalent between the two diets, clearances in all studies showed varying decreases in creatinine clearance with plant-based protein diets, indicating the kidneys did not have to work as hard with a change to plant-based protein sources. The reason for this is unclear, but it is theorized that the amino acid profile of the two protein sources is the rationale. In addition, it is found that most animal protein diets are overall higher in protein, which also is a burden to kidney filtering function, thus decreasing clearances.

There are only a few cautions to eating a high quality plant protein. The balance of amino acids can be unbalanced and could result in some deficiencies if you were to eat all grains for your protein. So, in order to maximize your amino acids profile, eating a variety of high plant-protein is recommended. This includes foods such as dried cooked beans and legumes, soy products and a variety of quality protein grains. This will be further explained in Chapter 6.

Myth #2: Vegetarian diets cannot provide you with enough protein

Over 50% of the world population meets their protein needs by grains alone. 65% of the world population meets their protein needs by plant proteins alone. Plant proteins can meet all your protein requirements. Plant proteins can provide a quality diet when a low protein diet is required. The only time you may need additional help with making sure you are getting enough nutritional balance from your vegetarian diet is if your kidney function is less than 29% and your are not on renal replacement therapy (RRT), such as dialysis. In this case, you may require the help of a Registered Dietitian, specializing in kidney disease, to plan a diet to meet your nutritional needs adequately.

Myth #3 Vegetarian diets are too high in phosphorus and potassium to be
used in kidney disease

Some plant proteins are higher in phosphorus than animal proteins. The
higher phosphorus content of these foods though is not as well absorbed as
from animal proteins. This occurs because many plant proteins are high in
a substance called phytates, which blocks the absorption of phosphorus.

Potassium in certain plant proteins such as nuts and beans is high. However,
these foods have other nutrients that can be of benefit to your kidney disease
treatment. With careful planning, all of your favorite foods can be worked
into your kidney disease diet.

Chapter Two
The Stages of Kidney Disease

THE STAGES OF KIDNEY FAILURE

There are two classifications of kidney failure, acute and chronic. Acute kidney failure happens very rapidly. You are often hospitalized, treated and usually regain kidney function. Diet changes needed for acute kidney failure are usually temporary and may be required in the acute phase only. Some benefit though from a continued vegetarian lifestyle can help you maintain your health and immunity to prevent further kidney damage. This diet is low in sodium and optimum for health and disease prevention.

This book is written to address the needs to the second type of kidney failure, chronic kidney disease. This is a progressive type of kidney failure that does not improve. However, with proper medical treatment chronic kidney disease can be slowed down or stopped from progressing. Nutrition is a very important part of that care.

CHRONIC KIDNEY DISEASE - BEFORE DIALYSIS

Renal insufficiency is when you have kidney function that is greater than 10% but less than 90%. Even though diet restriction of protein and other minerals only becomes needed at 50% function or less, you can begin a slightly lower protein, along with a lower sodium diet earlier. Research has shown a low protein diet in the very early stages of kidney disease may be most effective in slowing the progression of your disease. As stated, if you have been diagnosed with kidney disease and have less than 50% kidney function, you will definitely benefit from a slightly lower protein diet along with modifying other minerals. The amount of protein you require will depend on your level of kidney function. This is determined by your creatinine clearance, a test that indicates how well your kidneys are filtering. Check with your physician to find out your percent kidney function. When you know this you can determine what nutrients you need to watch in your diet.

END STAGE RENAL DISEASE

When your kidney function drops below 10-15 % you are now categorized as having end stage renal disease. This means that you can no longer sustain your life without renal replacement therapy, of which your choices are dialysis treatment or transplantation. If you are on dialysis, your diet needs become even more specific because your kidneys are no longer able to filter nutrients effectively. As a result, you need to limit certain minerals. It becomes important to eat a quality diet to stay as healthy as possible, while watching the intake of these minerals discussed in this book. The next chapter will help you determine and plan your diet if you have renal insufficiency or are on dialysis.

Chapter Three
The Kidney-Diet Link

WHAT HAS DIET GOT TO DO WITH OUR KIDNEYS

Three to seven million Americans have chronic kidney disease, with over 80, 000 people diagnosed every year. There are many causes to this disease. But whether your disease was brought on by genetics, a virus or from other reasons, what you eat or do not eat impacts your disease process. Until recently vegetarianism was thought to have a negative impact on your kidney disease. But we now know vegetarianism is a eating lifestyle that can help, not hinder, the progression of your disease

When you have kidney disease your body develop uremia or the build up of waste products in the blood. One of these waste products is urea nitrogen, a by-product of protein metabolism. If you eat too much protein, or protein that is thought to be" low value protein," the urea nitrogen level will build up sooner. In addition, several minerals you take for granted in your food are not filtered from the body efficiently and can affect your disease. These include sodium, potassium, calcium and phosphorus.

Even though your kidneys are no bigger than the size of your fist, they have many functions, such as controlling anemia, bone formation, high blood pressure and have effects on blood vessels and your heart. A large part of the function of the kidney and how it interacts with these factors is affected by what you eat.

PROTEIN

To build new tissues and replace old damaged tissues the body uses protein as the building blocks for this process. Sources of protein from vegetables include: beans, legumes, lentils, soy, grain and meat substitutes, also known as meat analogues. If you are lacto-ovo vegetarian dairy products such as milk, cheese and eggs also provide quality protein. By balancing protein in your diet you can minimize your blood level of urea nitrogen, feel better and delay some of the complications of your disease, while still maintaining the growth of your tissues.

PHOSPHORUS

Another function of the kidney involves bone health. When the kidney filtering begins to decrease, your body retains a mineral called phosphorus. As the level of phosphorus rises, it begins to pull calcium from the bones.

This is the body's natural way of trying to lower the levels. This can make the bones weaker. Recent research indicates this condition can contribute to heart disease as well. So in addition to watching protein, you may need to limit phosphorus-containing foods, as a low phosphorus diet may help slow down kidney damage and these complications.

Phosphorus is found in almost all foods but it is especially high in animal proteins, milk, cheese, cottage cheese, and yogurt. (See Table 1) Some plant-based proteins though such as beans and nuts are also high in phosphorus. But by carefully balancing your choice of these foods and the amounts, you can work these foods into your diet.

Often limiting foods high in phosphorus is not enough and you make require a medication called phosphorus binders. These medications are taken when you eat to bind up the phosphorus by working in your digestive track before the phosphorus enters your blood stream. The extra phosphorus then passes out of your body through the stool.

PHOSPHORUS
Table 1

Limiting yourself to **one** of the following foods per day will best help you in keeping the amount of phosphorus in your blood at a normal level.

HIGH PHOSPHORUS CONTAINING FOODS	
• Milk (8 ounces or 1 cup)	• Pizza (1/4 of 12 inch pizza)
• Cheese (2 ounces)	• Nuts (1/2 cup or 2 ounces)
• Cottage cheese (3/4 cup)	• Waffle: frozen or mix (2 squares)
• Ice cream (1 1/2 cup)	• Pancakes (2 medium)
• Pudding:	• Macaroni and cheese (1 cup)
Instant (1/2 cup)	• Bran cereals:
Homemade (1 cup)	All Bran (1/3 cup)
• Custard (1 cup)	100% Bran (1/3 cup)
• Yogurt (1 cup)	Bran Buds (1/3 cup)

CALCIUM

When following a low phosphorus diet you may not get enough calcium, as many foods high in phosphorus also contain calcium. Therefore, many people on a low phosphorus diet require a calcium supplement. Your blood can be tested to see what your level for calcium is and to determine what you need. Do not start taking a calcium supplement without talking to your physician first because if you supplement yourself without first checking, your level could get dangerously high.

SODIUM

Most people with kidney disease require a low sodium diet. Normally, when you eat the mineral sodium, your kidneys get rid of what your body does not need. When your kidneys are not working well, sodium builds up in your body, which in turn can cause an elevated blood pressure.

The sodium in your diet comes from both the food you eat and the salt you add. Salt (sodium chloride) is 40% sodium and you should avoid using it on your food. Foods that contains a lot of sodium and should be avoided are canned soup, pickles, some of the meat substitutes, snack foods, processed cheese, frozen meals, soy sauce, seasoning salt and fast foods. For most of us, an occasional high sodium food is desirable. Table 2 gives examples of these high sodium foods and how you can work them into your diet on occasion.

Keep in mind, when you start limiting how much salt you eat, foods may taste different. On average it will take 3 weeks to lose the taste for excess sodium in the food you eat. Try using herbs or the no salt seasoning blends from the grocery store, to improve the taste of your food (See Table 3).

*HIGH SODIUM FOODS
Table 2

CHEESE
Processed cheeses and
Cheese spreads (1oz or 2 tbs.)

SOUPS
Bouillon cubes (1)
Regular canned, dried or
frozen soup (1/2 cup)
Miso sauce (1/4 c)

VEGETABLES
Frozen vegetables with prepared
sauces (1/2 cup)
Sauerkraut (1/4 cup)
Olives (5)
Pickle (1)

CONDIMENTS AND
SEASONINGS
Seasonings that contain "salt" or
"sodium"
in their name (i.e. celery salt,
garlic salt,
onion salt) (1/8 tsp.)
Catsup (3 tbs.)
Meat tenderizer (1/8 tsp.)
Monosodium glutamate (MSG)
(1/8 tsp.)
Soy sauce (1 1/2 tsp.)
-Worcestershire sauce (3 tbs.)
Salt (1/8 tsp.)

FAST FOODS
Pizza (2 slices)
Mexican (1 entree)
Chinese (1 entree)

CONVENIENCE ITEMS
Commercial mixes for:
Gravies (1/4 c)
Sauces (i.e. spag. sauce, au jus, etc.
1/4 c)
Noodles, rice, stuffing, and potatoes
(1/2 c)

SNACK FOODS
Corn chips, potato chips, pretzels
(1 c)
Salted nuts (1/2 c)
Salted crackers (10)
Party dips and spreads (1/4 c)

*These foods contain 500-1000 mg per serving. Limit their use to no more than once per day in the
portion identified

BLENDS AND OTHER SEASONINGS TO TRY INSTEAD OF SALT
TABLE 3

Apple pie spice	Bell pepper flakes	Bouillon (salt & potassium free)
Celery flakes	Celery leaves	
Cinnamon sugar	Curry	Chili powder
Garlic	Honey	Fine herbs
Italian seasoning	Leeks	Horseradish (fresh)
Molasses	Onions	Lemon (juice, peel)
Pickling spice	Pimento	Onion flakes or powder
Pumpkin pie spice	Sugar	Poultry seasoning
Vinegar	Watercress	Vegetable flakes
Wright's liquid smoke	Veg-it	Wine
Mrs. Dash	Papa Dash	

COMMERCIAL LOW SODIUM PRODUCTS

There are several low sodium spice mixtures on the market to choose from, but you need to be careful in your selection. Avoid mixtures that contain salt or sodium as one of the first four ingredients on the label. If you are on a potassium-restricted diet avoid spices mixtures that contain potassium chloride as one of the first four ingredients.

Some of the more popular companies that produce low sodium and low potassium spice blends are:

Akzo Salt, Inc. 717-587-9525

Alberto Culver Mrs. Dash 1-800-622-3274

Lawrys Foods, Inc. 1-800-952-9797

Durkee 1-800-777-4959

McCormick 1-800-632-5847

Medi Diet Mrs. Dash/Papa Dash 1-800-MEDDIET

Minors 1-800-827-8328

POTASSIUM

As kidney failure progresses you may need to watch your intake of another mineral, potassium. Normally when you eat potassium, your kidneys get rid of what your body does not need. When your kidneys are not working well, they may not get rid of this excess potassium so it builds up in your blood. Potassium is involved in muscle contraction, and if the balance of your potassium goes too high or too low, your muscles can become very weak. The most important muscle this can affect is your heart. This can be dangerous. If this happens, you will require a potassium restricted diet. However, this often does not occur unless your kidney function is less than 20% or you are requiring dialysis treatments.

Potassium is found in all foods, but is most concentrated in fruits, vegetables and juices. For that reason these are the foods that need to be limited on potassium restricted diet. Table 4 lists these foods into categories of high, medium and low amounts of potassium. When requiring a potassium restricted diet, most people can do quite well with limiting themselves to one of the HIGH potassium foods per day, no more than 2 from the MEDIUM potassium foods and no more than 3 from the LOW potassium foods per day.

POTASSIUM FOOD LIST
Table 4

HIGH POTASSIUM
(250-500MG)

FRUITS

Apricots (3)

Avocados (1/4)

Bananas (1)

Dates (5)

Figs (3)

Kiwi (1)

Melons: cantaloupe,
honeydew (1/4 of 5″ diameter)

Nectarines (1)

Oranges (1)

Papayas (1)

Prunes (5)

Raisins (1/4 cup)

Tangelo (1)

Watermelon (6″ x 1″ slice)

VEGETABLES

Artichokes (1)

Beans: kidney, lima, navy,
pinto (1/2 cup)

Nuts: all kinds (1/2 cup)

Parsnips (1/2 cup)

Potatoes (1/2 cup or 1/2 of
medium or 10 French fries)

Pumpkin (1/2 cup)

Spinach, cooked (1/2 cup)

Split peas, black-eyed peas,
lentils (1/2 cup)

Tomatoes (1)

Tomato sauce (1/4 cup)

Winter squash (1/2 cup)

Yams, sweet potatoes (1/2 c)

MEDIUM POTASSIUM
(150-250MG)

FRUITS

Apple (1 small or 1/2 of large)

Cherries (1/2 cup or 15)

Fruit cocktail (1/2 cup)

Grapefruit (1/2)

Peaches, canned (1/2 c)

Peaches, fresh (1)

Pears, fresh (1 sm. or 1/2 large)

Plums (2)

VEGETABLES

Broccoli (1/2 cup)

Brussels sprouts (1/2 cup)

Beets (1/2 cup)

Carrots (1/2 cup)

Celery (1/2 cup)

Greens, cooked:

beet, chard, collard, mustard,

turnip (1/2 cup)

Eggplant (1/2 cup)

Mixed vegetables (1/2 cup)

Mushrooms, raw (1/2 cup)

Okra (1/2 cup or 10 pods)

Peanut butter (2 tbs.)

Peppers (1 or 1/2 cups)

Potato chips (unsalted) (10)

LOW POTASSIUM
(100-150MG)

FRUITS

Applesauce (1/2 cup)

Blackberries (1/2 cup)

Blueberries (1/2 cup)

Cranberries (1 cup)

Grapes (1/2 cup or 15)

Pears, canned (1/2 cup)

Pineapple (1/2 cup)

Plums, canned (1/2 cup or 3)

Raspberries (1/2 cup)

Rhubarb, cooked (1/2 cup)

Strawberries (1/2 cup)

Tangerines (1)

VEGETABLES

Asparagus (4 spears)

Beans: green / wax (1/2 cup)

Bean sprouts (1/2 cup)

Cabbage (1/2 cup)

Cauliflower (1/2 cup)

Corn (1/2 cup)

Cucumber (1/2 cup)

Lettuce (1 cup)

Onions (1/2 cup)

Peas: green (1/2 cup)

Radishes (5)

Rutabagas, cooked (1/2 cup)

Soaked potatoes (1/2 cup)

Summer squash (1/2 cup)

Turnips (1/2 cup)

Water chestnuts (4)

HIGH POTASSIUM (250-500MG)	MEDIUM POTASSIUM (150-250MG)	LOW POTASSIUM (100-150MG)
JUICES	**JUICES**	**JUICES**
Orange juice (1/2 cup)	Apple juice (1/2 cup)	Cranapple juice (1 cup)
Prune juice (1/2 cup)	Apricot nectar (1/2 cup)	Cranberry juice (1 cup)
Tomato juice, (1/2 cup)	Grape juice, canned (1/2 cup)	Crangrape juice (1 cup)
V-8 juice (1/2 cup)	Grapefruit juice (1/2 cup)	Grape juice, frozen (1 cup)
	Pineapple juice (1/2 cup)	Hi-C /Fruit drinks (1 cup)
		Kool-Aid (1 cup)
		Lemonade /Limeade (1 cup)
		Peach nectar (1/2 cup)
		Pear nectar (1 cup)
		Tang (1 cup)

FAT

Fat often gets a bad reputation. From unwanted calories to heart disease, it has often been identified as the food culprit. It is true excess fat remains a health hazard, but amidst this obsession that people have with using fat free food the less publicized benefits of fats should not be ignored. With kidney disease you need 15-30 % of your calories from fat and if you have heart disease, high blood pressure or a high cholesterol level, you still should have at least 10-20% of your daily calories as fat.

The key to eating fat is eating the right kind. There is saturated, polyunsaturated and monosaturated fats. While saturated fats are very plentiful, giving us the pleasure of enjoying many cream sauces, pastries, desserts or flavorful snack foods, these fats can play havoc with your health. A high saturated fat diet can contribute to heart disease and possibly certain kind of cancers. Certain polyunsaturated fats that are also plentiful in our foods such as hydrogenated fats, corn oil or safflower oil products and trans fatty acids, like we find in stick margarine, are not health enhancing. There are other fats with far more health benefits. Two of these are Omega 3, known as an essential fat and the other is monosaturated fat.

Essential Fats:

Our body can produce most of the fats we need, so we do not even need to eat them. The exception is linolenic and linoleic acid or Omega 6 and Omega 3 fats. Omega 6 are commonly found in many vegetables oils, margarine and other packaged foods. However, Omega 3 fats are far less available. This is because they are so unsaturated they cannot be used in cooking and they have a very short shelf life.

Omega 3 fats have been found to be especially beneficial in two types of kidney disease, IgA Nephropathy, and lupus, but in all types of kidney disease Omega 3 can be beneficial. Nuts, flaxseed, flaxseed oil are good sources of Omega 3 fatty acids. The key is making sure you add in the Omega 3 to off set an excess of Omega 6 fats. Getting in one serving of Omega 3 fats a day should accomplish this.

This list below shows some Omega 3 foods and what is a serving size:

1 cup soy milk

2 tablespoon flaxseed

2 tablespoons flaxseed oil

4 oz tofu-not the low fat kind

¼ cup walnuts

Monosaturated

Monosaturated fats, known as Omega 9 fats, though not essential, are important to your health. These fats help reduce your bad cholesterol called low-density lipoproteins (LDL). Decreasing LDL is important in decreasing your risk for heart disease. By substituting monosaturated fats like olive oil for more harmful fats you can be assured of a good mix of the right fats.

The right balance of fats can reduce some of the complications of kidney disease such as heart disease and high fat or lipid levels in the blood. In addition, Omega 3 fats have been associated with improving the body's ability to fight infection. Research has shown an additional benefit in treating skin disorders that are associated with kidney disease, and with less intake of saturated fat and more Omega 3 fats.

TYPES OF FAT IN YOUR DIET
Table 5

SATURATED FAT SOURCES	POLYUNSATURATED FAT SOURCES	MONOSATURATED FAT SOURCES
Found in: meats, dairy products, butter, milk, ice cream, coconut, palm and palm kernel oils.	Omega 6 Fats: safflower, sunflower, corn, soybean and cottonseed oils and some fish. Omega 3 fats- coldwater wild fish, soy products, flaxseed oils, canola oils, soybean oil, walnuts and flaxseeds	Olive oil Canola oil Avocado Peanut oil Flaxseed oil
Cholesterol is a fat-like substance produced by the livers of all animals: beef, pork, poultry, fish, milk products and eggs. Only found in foods of animal origin.		
Fried foods		
Trans-fatty acids- stick margarine		
Hydrogenated fats- processed foods, packaged pastries, cookies and cakes		

CALORIES

When changing your diet you often need to reduce the amount of certain foods or eliminate foods you were used to eating. As a result, you will need to replace those foods with others so that you do not decrease your calories and lose weight. This is especially important when following a low protein diet. You may need to add extra fats or oils to your food, as you give more attention to your servings of carbohydrates. If your body does not get enough calories it will use the protein you eat for energy instead of using it for building or maintaining vital tissues. Chapter 7 goes into further detail on adding calories.

It is common when your kidney function is low not to feel like eating. Taste changes and some nausea may make food less desirable. For this reason you need to watch your weight and make sure you are not losing. Weight loss can depress your immune system and cause you to be more susceptible to infections and other illnesses. Be sure to add extra fats and use the maximum number of servings in each group you are allowed. If you are still losing weight you may benefit from a nutritional supplement that supplies extra calories. This needs to be selected with caution based on your level of kidney function. Many of these products are high in potassium, phosphorus and protein, which may be dangerous to your health. Because of this, you should consult with a Registered Dietitian to determine the most appropriate supplement for you.

On the other hand eating too many calories can contribute to weight gain. This is a health hazard in chronic disease. If you are overeating or gaining too much weight, stay to the lower end of the servings in the food lists. In addition, keep your fat servings to a minimum.

HOW IS THE DIET DIFFERENT FOR EACH STAGE OF KIDNEY DISASE

Because everyone is different in how their kidney disease effects them, it is highly recommend that you check with your physician on which minerals are important or are a concern for your specific medical conditions. The following table below reviews the typical diet guidelines required for different stages of kidney disease.

DETERMINING YOUR DIET NEEDS Table 6		
NUTRIENT	**PREDIALYSIS**	**DIALYSIS**
Protein	Varies	Not restricted
Phosphorus	Varies	Restricted
Calcium	Varies	Supplements restricted
Sodium	Restricted	Restricted
Potassium	Varies	Restricted
Calories	Not restricted	Not restricted
Fluid	Not restricted	Restricted

Chapter Four
Making Your Diet Plan

PUTTING IT ALL TOGETHER

Putting your diet together is key to giving you nutritional balance. The following pages will give you an outline to pick the amount of protein you need and the correct servings of the foods to include in your diet. The groups are: MILK, phosphorus containing foods, PROTEIN, FRUIT and VEGETABLES, GRAINS and BREADS, and FAT. Each group has been broken down into good choices and those that are not so good or to slow down on. The foods in the SLOW DOWN group are going to be higher in sodium or hydrogenated fats. Included under each food group name is the number of servings to have each day. The second column is the good choices of foods in that category and the appropriate servings sizes and in the SLOW DOWN column are foods that would not be recommended. Following in Table 7 is further explanation of the different food groups.

FOOD GROUP	GOOD CHOICES &SERVING SIZE	SLOW DOWN
MILK 1 Serving	1 cup milk 1 cup yogurt 2 oz cheese ¾ cup pudding, ¾ cup custard ¾ cup cottage cheese 2 cups soy milk	Processed cheese
QUALITY PROTEIN See Chart p 26 For individualized recommended serving(s)	1 egg ¼ cup Tuno 2 oz tofu 1 oz seitan ¼ cup meatless ground meat 1/3 cup dry cooked beans (limit to 2 servings per day)	
FRUITS/ VEGETABLES 5-6 Servings	½ cup cooked or fresh vegetables 1 small fresh or ½ cup canned fruit or ½ cup juice ½ cup low sodium tomato or V-8 juice 3 tablespoons peanut butter ¼ cup nuts– preferably flaxseeds, walnuts or pumpkin ¼ avocado	Pickled vegetables, such as sauerkraut or dill pickles
FATS	1 tablespoon butter or soft tub margarine 2 tablespoon cream cheese 1 tablespoon oil– olive or canola preferred for cooking	Fats in commercially prepared food
MISCELLANEOUS FOODS	**Jam/jelly *Honey Lemon juice *Kool-Aid **Soda pop **Popsicles *Cream mints *Hard candy *Jelly beans *Lolly pops Cornstarch Herbs/Spices *Sugar/Syrup Vinegar Wheat Starch Coffee/Tea Rice Dream-Unenriched	Salt Salt substitutes Convenience foods i.e. soups, stews, frozen meals or casseroles(unless low sodium)

YOUR DAILY DIET PLAN
Table 7

* Avoid these foods if you have diabetes and discuss how to include these in your meal with a Registered Dietitian or Certified Diabetes Educator

**Use sugar substitute alternative if you have diabetes

MILK

Milk and other dairy products are high in the mineral phosphorus. You should begin limiting your phosphorus foods when your kidney function is 50% or less, EVEN IF YOUR BLOOD LEVEL FOR PHOSPHORUS IS NORMAL. Early on in kidney disease too much phosphorus can stimulate your parathyroid gland to produce a hormone that when produced in excess can cause too much calcium to be pulled from your bones. Ultimately this process can cause bone disease.

You cannot eliminate all phosphorus in your diet, but you can limit dairy products, meat and dark colored carbonated beverages, which are the most concentrated sources of this mineral. There are other non-dairy, non-meat foods that are also high in phosphorus and occasionally have to be minimized if your blood phosphorus level is elevated. When you are limiting dairy there are many substitutes for milk. These include soymilk, rice milk and non-dairy creamers. Soymilk and rice milk are preferred to the non-dairy creamers because they have other health benefits and are also lower in concentrated sugars and devoid of saturated fats. Table 8 outlines a list of some of the more common milk substitutes.

MILK AND MILK SUBSTITUTES Table 8 (Cup servings)							
Product	Calories	Protein (mg)	Fat (gm)	Sodium (mg)	Potassium (mg)	Phosphorus (mg)	Milk Equiv.
Milk, 2%	121	8.1	4.7	122	377	234	1
Mocha Mix	305	<1	25	158	320	130	2
Mocha Mix: Light	160	<1	12	68	290	120	2
Soy Milk: Creamy	160-210	7-9	7	130-180	210-450	160	2
Light	90-130	4	2	95-130	100-200	100-125	2
Rice Dream: Original	134	<1	3	70	15	15	0

Non-Dairy Creamers

Non-dairy creamer is made from vegetable oil, instead of milk fat. It can be a substitute for half and half because it has the same consistency. Non-dairy creamer also contains some corn syrup and as a result is very sweet in taste. This product is found in most grocery stores.

Soy Milk

Soymilk is made from soybeans. It is higher in protein than non-dairy creamer or rice milk. When compared to non-dairy creamers, the "light" brands have a lower in fat content. Soymilk comes in original, vanilla, and cocoa flavors. (CAUTION: the cocoa flavors are high in potassium). Soymilk can be used as a direct replacement for milk in cooking or baking (custards, white sauces, and soups), but not in pudding mixes. This product is available in grocery stores and health food stores.

Rice Milk

Rice milk is made from brown rice and safflower oil. It comes in two types, original and enriched. Original is lower in phosphorus and potassium and can be used freely in your diet. Rice milk can be used as a direct replacement in cooking or baking in place of milk. This product is mainly found in health food stores but frequently is being found is grocery stores.

Cooking with Milk Substitutes

Non-dairy creamers should be diluted, 3 parts water to 1 part non-dairy creamer, in cooking. Soymilk and rice milk can be used directly in recipes requiring milk. NOTES: Milk substitutes cannot be used in place of milk in all situations. For example, these substitutes will not make "sour milk". Instant pudding needs the acid in milk, which is not present in these products. Therefore, pudding needs to be made from scratch if using any of the milk substitute products.

PROTEINS:

The amount of protein you require will depend upon your level of kidney function. Excluding the Protein Group, your diet plan is estimated to provide you with about 25 grams of protein. Quality vegetable protein should provide 50% of your protein needs. The chart below will help you determine how many servings of quality vegetable protein you will require every day, based on your level of kidney function, to meet all your protein needs.

KIDNEY FUNCTION
protein servings you need per day

wt in kg	50-100%	25-50%	<25% *	Requiring HD	Requiring PD
40	2	2	*	3	3.5
50	2.5	2.5	*	4	6
60	3	3	*	6	7
70	5	5	*	7.5	8
80	6	6	*	9	10
90	7	7	*	10	12
100	8	8	*	12	13

HD = hemodialysis
PD= peritoneal dialysis
*At this level of kidney function it is recommended that you be followed by a Registered Dietitian who specializes in kidney disease

Vegetarian protein foods are easily divided into three groups: bean and legumes, soy proteins and meat analogues. The exception to this is seitan, which is a grain-based protein from gluten, which is very concentrated in protein.

Beans and legumes

This group of vegetable proteins offers fiber, isoflavones and trace minerals. Many experts in the field of kidney disease may group all beans together, having the same protein, phosphorus, and potassium content. But actually beans vary in their nutrient content. Initially, you can treat all beans the same. However, if you start to have more specific problems such as a high potassium or high phosphorus, you may need to be more specific in the beans and legumes you select. . For example, if your potassium is high, you may need to limit lentils and instead eat adzuki beans. If your phosphorus is high you may need to switch to more lupin beans. Appendix C is a breakdown of some of the more common beans and legumes and their nutrient compositions.

Soy proteins

Soy has become very popular in recent years. Most of these products can fit well into your diet. Tofu, tempeh, soymilk, soy nuts and soybeans are all soy foods. Many meat analogues are high in soy or what is called soy isolates. Ideally soy is where you should get the bulk of your vegetable protein. Research has shown soy proteins to be very effective in slowing down protein loss through your urine, preserving kidney function, lowering high blood pressure, and reducing the risks of heart disease. Certain soy-based proteins are worth mentioning, though, as being less desirable. These include Natto, which is high in potassium, Miso, which is high in sodium and soybeans which are high in potassium and phosphorus. Even though occasional use of these foods would be acceptable, they should be discouraged on a regular basis.

Meat Analogues

Meat analogues are the pool of vegetarian foods made from a variety of plant sources. For many, these products taste and look a lot like meat. Mainly containing soy, these foods can contain grains, nuts, seeds and beans or legumes. Most of these work well in a kidney disease diet, except they tend to be much higher in sodium. For several of these products, the phosphorus content is not known or is not analyzed by the manufacturer. However, if the food is low in beans or dairy, you can usually be guaranteed it is fairly low in phosphorus. Refer to Appendix E for a list of the more common meat analogues and their nutrient composition. The ones listed are most appropriate for people with kidney disease with the exception of Green Giant's Harvest Burgers and Boca Burgers. The potassium is quite high in these products but is listed due to their availability in most grocery stores.

Seitan

Seitan is a vegetable protein made from wheat gluten. It is firm, has a meaty texture, and works well in stews and casseroles as a replacement for meat. A diet very high in this protein though would lack certain amino acids and not be good, but using no more than ½ of your protein for this type of food is acceptable

Fruit and Vegetables

Fruits and vegetables are often given a bad reputation with kidney disease, mainly because these foods are high in potassium. But in spite of this, these foods are very important in your long-term health, because they are high in many antioxidants, phytochemicals, minerals, vitamins and fiber. The key is selecting fruits and vegetables that are highest in nutrients that benefit your health, while minimizing the nutrients that are of concern. Most people with kidney disease do not need to start limiting their dietary intake of potassium until their kidney function is below 20%. But even if your function is above 20% it is important to have your potassium level checked regularly to determine that it is in the normal range. Often with kidney disease, the regulatory system for maintaining a normal potassium level in the blood is malfunctioning. If you eat too much potassium your body may not get rid of it and you can become very ill. If you do not eat enough potassium or become ill with diarrhea or vomiting your potassium level may go too low. Diuretics are used to treat hypertension and help maintain the body balance of water as the kidney function declines. These medications can also affect potassium balance.

The symptoms of too much and too little potassium are often the same. You can get weakness in the legs and, if not treated or corrected, the weakness can spread to the upper body. Some people describe an "achy" feeling like the flu. Further, if not treated, a high potassium can cause heart irregularities and actually stop the heart. This is why potassium regulation is so important in both chronic kidney disease (CKD) and end stage renal disease (ESRD).

Refer to the Potassium Guidelines on page 16 and 17 if you require more restriction in your potassium containing foods. Also in following Your Daily Meal Plan guidelines, select a variety of colors in fruits and vegetables. This will ensure you are getting a range of nutrients.

Bread and Grains

Grains are often thought to be a complement to a meal but not the source of protein in a meal. They used to be thought of as "incomplete" according to the old standards for evaluation protein quality. The newer standards of evaluation reveal these foods can be very complete and can add quality protein if included in a mixed diet of other foods such as tofu, beans or dairy products. The problem with grains is by themselves they lack certain amino acids, but when mixed with other foods they can become a balanced protein source. This was seen in studies of Indian tribes who only lived off millet. They were found to have an unbalanced protein profile, but when the millet was mixed with other foods the profile of amino acids became complete.

Not only are many grains high in protein, they have other nutrients that have a very important role in your diet planning. The chart that follows lists some of the better grains to select and their nutrient content. Note that rice and barley are some of the lower potassium grains, whereas quinoa is higher in potassium and needs to be watched closer if you require potassium restriction. Grains are high in trace minerals. Extra supplementation of trace minerals in kidney disease is not recommended. Getting these trace minerals from your diet runs less risk of toxicity while providing you with the benefit of receiving nutrients.

NUTRIENT CONTENT OF BREAD AND GRAINS TABLE 9				
GRAINS (½ CUP COOKED or 4 OZ PORTIONS)	CALORIES	PROTEIN	POTASSIUM	PHOSPHORUS
RICE-BROWN	100	5	153	151
RICE-WHITE	130	5	60	70
QUINOA	120	5	209	NA
COUSCOUS	100	3	50	20
BULGAR	75	3	65	35
MILLETT	120	4	75	120
SEITAN	70	15	46	NA
BARLEY	100	3	128	NA

FATS

You need fat. Fat provides concentrated calories and fundamental nutrients to your diet. Like mentioned in Chapter 3, there are good fats and not so good fats. Your body requires the two essential fats to stay healthy. These fats are omega 6 and omega 3 fatty acids. Omegas 6 are very plentiful in most diets, found in such foods as cooking oils and margarines. Omega 3 fatty acids are less plentiful but are critical to your health, especially when you have kidney disease. You should have at least one serving of these foods every day such as firm tofu, walnuts, flaxseed oil, flaxseed or soymilk (not fat free). In certain kinds of kidney disease such as polycystic kidney disease or lupus it is paramount to consume omega 3 fatty acids every day. Research has shown polycystic cysts have decreased with the use of omega

3 fatty acids. Lupus patients have improved with a delay in kidney damage by increasing omega 3 fatty acids. See Chapter 3 for details on these fats.

Please note flaxseed oil SHOULD NOT BE USED IN COOKING. It is a very perishable fat and if heated will oxidize and taste bitter, in addition to turning from an anti-oxidant to a pro-oxidant! This is harmful to your health, which is not what you want. If you are hungry or need extra calories, it may be important to add servings to the fat group so you do not lose weight. However, if you are gaining too much weight you may want to minimize the less desirable fat choices.

Chapter Five
Kidney Disease and Other Diseases

DIABETES AND KIDNEY DISEASE

Over 50% of kidney disease is due to diabetes. If you have both diabetes and kidney disease, you can feel a little overwhelmed. You may wonder what there is, if anything, to eat! Actually the diabetic and kidney diet can be quite easily combined. One of the best ways to delay the progression of kidney disease is to control your blood sugar. Blood sugar monitoring is recommended for all people with diabetes, whether on oral medications, insulin or diet alone. For maintaining good blood sugar control is the best way to avoid complications related to diabetes and kidney disease.

Here are 4 key tips to help you:

1.<u>Keep track of your blood sugar</u>

If you are on dialysis or if your kidney function is below 30% you may begin to notice changes in how much insulin you require. This is because your kidney is no longer able to process and eliminate insulin, and as a result it stays in your body longer. Keeping track of changes in your blood sugar and your insulin reactions will help you and your doctor make the best adjustments in your insulin dosage.

2. <u>Keep meals regular</u>

No matter what your schedule is, a regular routine is best. For times when you are tired or busy, keep easy to fix foods on hand. If you are sick or nauseated you still need to eat. This will keep your blood sugar stable. Keep liquid drinks or foods on hand that are easy for you to digest.

3. <u>Keep your carbohydrates consistent</u>

Making sure the amount of insulin you take is appropriate for the amount of carbohydrates you take in is very important to your long-term health. Breads, grains, fruits and vegetables provide varying degrees of carbohydrate. See the table following. Making sure that the amounts of these foods are consistent from meal to meal will help stabilize your blood sugar.

CARBOHYDRATE SOURCES		
FOOD GROUP	SERVINGS	CARBOHYDRATE (grams)
BREAD	1	15
FRUIT	1	15
MILK	8 oz	12
VEGETABLES	½ cup cooked 1 cup raw	5
GRAINS	½ cup	15

4. Keep Easy to Prepare Foods for Nausea

The following is a list of foods easily tolerated by most people when they are sick.. Each food will provide 15 grams of carbohydrate in the serving size listed. To get 150-200 grams of carbohydrate for one day, choose at least 10 foods below. It is a good idea to do have some of these foods on hand in case you were to get sick.

BREAD AND STARCHES

1 slice bread

½ cup hot cereal

6 each crackers (Ritz, Hi Ho or saltines)

3 graham crackers (2-1/2 inch square)

6 each vanilla wafers

1 small baked potato

½ cup mashed potatoes

1 oz unsalted pretzels

1/3 cup rice

<u>Milk or Milk Substitute Products</u>

¼ cup milkshake

1 ½ cups Tofu Milkshake (see Chapter 8 Recipes)

¼ cup pudding-regular

½ cup pudding low calorie

½ cup ice cream

½ cup eggnog - commercial

1cup milk

1 ½ cups soymilk

1cup plain yogurt or artificially sweetened yogurt

<u>Fruit juices and other sweets</u>

½ cup fruit juice

½ cup unsweetened applesauce

½ cup regular soft drink

½ twin Popsicle

1 tablespoon regular jams or jellies

1 tablespoon white or granular sugar

1 tablespoon honey

¼ cup sherbet

1 cup cream soup

½ cup regular gelatin

½ can Resource or Ensure Diabetic

SAMPLE MENU FOR CARBOHYDRATE REPLACEMENT WHEN YOU ARE SICK

<u>1st meal</u>

½ cup hot cereal 15 grams

1 cup milk or 1 ½ cup

soy milk 15 grams

1 tablespoon sugar 15 grams

<u>2nd meal</u>

4 oz 7-up 15 grams

<u>3rd meal</u>

½ cup apple juice 15 grams

8 animal crackers 15 grams

<u>4th meal</u>

1 cup cream soup 15 grams

<u>5th meal</u>

¼ cup pudding 15 grams

<u>6th meal</u>

½ cup 7 up 15 grams

1 piece dry toast 15 grams

Total 150 grams

5. Know what to do if your blood sugar drops low

Test your blood sugar often. If your blood sugar goes low use sugar in water or regular pop or soda to treat. DO NOT use juice if you can avoid it. Juice is high in potassium and may cause your potassium to go too high.

A blood sugar less than 70 mg/dl is considered a low blood sugar. This should be treated with readily available sugar, such as 3-5 lifesavers or ½ cup regular pop.

A blood sugar greater than 300 mg/dl is considered a high blood sugar. If this occurs, and you are not ill, try a little activity and recheck your blood sugar in 4 hours. If after 4 hours it is still greater than 300 mg/dl, you should contact your physician.

6. Know how to take your diabetes medications.

It is important to know the right time to take your diabetes medications. For this can impact the effectiveness of the medication and control of your blood sugars. Check with your doctor, pharmacist or dietitian if you are unsure.

HEART DISEASE

Sometimes it is hard to tell which came first, the kidney disease or the heart disease. Regardless, kidney disease can often be linked to circulatory and vascular heart disease. In addition, high cholesterol levels are a consistent feature of certain types of kidney disease and may be an important risk factor for progressive hardening of the arteries and thus the progression of kidney damage. Plant based diets are higher in fiber and lower in total fat, saturated fat and cholesterol than non vegetarian diets. Vegetarians in general have been found to have lower rates of heart disease and hypertension.

LIPID PROFILE

An important step in heart disease prevention is to know your lipid profile, the different types of fat in your blood. If you have not done so, or have not done so in a while, ask your physician for a lipid panel. The level of fat in your blood helps to determine your own personal risk for heart disease and stroke.

Type of Fat	Acceptable	Borderline	High-Risk
Cholesterol	Below 200	200-239	Greater than 240
HDL	Greater than 45	35-45	Less than 35
LDL	Less than 100	100-130	Greater than 130
Triglycerides	Less than 200	200-399	Greater than 400

Once you know your own lipid profile, you can begin to eat in a way to make your lipid profile as healthy as possible. Each type of fat you eat affects you're your lipids differently.

Saturated fats-Raises total cholesterol levels. *Limit saturated fats in your diet.*

Sources: Usually hard at room temperature. Animal fats and some vegetable fats such as coconut, palm oil and cocoa butter are high sources of saturated fat. Also found in hydrogenated fat (trans fatty acids) such as stick margarine, packaged pastries, cookies and cakes.

Polyunsaturated fats-Lowers total cholesterol, HDL and LDL

>   Sources: Found in most vegetable oils such as corn, safflower, soybean, sunflower, and cottonseed.

Monounsaturated fats-Lowers total cholesterol and LDL, does not affect HDL. *Use monounsaturated fats when you use fat in your diet*

>   Sources: Olive, canola, peanut oil, olives and most nuts (but high in potassium).

Omega-3 Fatty Acids-Lowers total cholesterol and LDL. *The American Heart Association recommends eating at least two servings per week to lower your risk of sudden cardiac death.*

>   Sources: Soymilk, firm tofu or flaxseed oil. Keep in mind though if you use flaxseed oil, that it cannot be used in cooking. It must be used cold. Flaxseed oil is very perishable when heated.

Small changes can impact your lipid profile. Look at the fats you are using in cooking, Try substituting canola oil or olive oil for hydrogenated fats. Replace your stick margarine with tub margarine. Try a stir-fry with peanut oil. Dip your bread in olive oil and balsamic vinegar instead of margarine. Sprinkle a few nuts or a few olives on a salad. Limit your use of packaged cookies, cakes and pastries. Mix flaxseed oil with your favorite salad dressing, or drizzle it over rice or pasta.

To help you follow both your vegetarian diet for kidney disease and your heart disease diet, also try to follow these tips:

- Choose low fat milk or milk substitute products

- Choose high fiber foods, such as fresh fruits and vegetables instead of canned, and whole grain breads instead of processed or white bread or grain products.

- If you are overweight, work with a renal dietitian in a weight loss program that is safe for you to follow.

CANCER

Not only can certain kinds of kidney disease be caused by cancer, treatments for cancer such as chemotherapy or radiation may cause kidney disease. The vegetarian diet is naturally higher in cancer fighting components. As a result vegetarianism will help keep your immune function stronger for your cancer prevention and treatment. To further assist you in maximizing your nutritional needs for both diseases, try to use as many fresh products as possible. Avoid a lot of processed types of vegetarian foods such as meat analogues or packaged vegetable dishes with added preservatives. If you are using milk products, chooses organic products. If you are receiving cancer treatment, now is not a time to lose weight. If you are losing weight unintentionally, work with a renal dietitian to help you meal plan for an adequate amount of nutrients for preventing further weight loss.

LUPUS AND KIDNEY DISEASE

Some of the first studies on vegetarianism and kidney disease were patients with lupus erythmetous. Research showed that lupus complications could be delayed or prevented with a plant based diet. The most important finding in the research was the use of omega 3 fatty acids in lupus and the benefit in the nutritional treatment with lupus.

POLYCYSTIC KIDNEY DISEASE

Polycystic kidney disease is a hereditary form of kidney disease. Fifty percent of people who have this disease never develop kidney failure. However, because this disease has the potential of progressing to kidney failure due to cyst formation on the kidneys, diet can be one way to slow down this risk. Most important is to avoid foods that can promote cyst formation and second is to avoid factors that can increase your blood pressure, which can affect kidney disease progression.

Caffeine and alcohol can promote cyst formation and should be avoided as much as possible. Some obvious sources of caffeine are coffee, tea and cola, and less obvious are chocolate, Anacin, and Exedrin. Carefully read labels on food and medications to avoid excess caffeine.

A vegetarian diet can also help slow down the progression of polycystic kidney failure. Studies have shown that soy products in general are beneficial in polycystic disease. In addition, increasing the use of omega 3 fatty acids and following a high potassium diet have also been found to be beneficial. A high potassium diet can only be followed as long as kidney function is greater than 20% and high potassium blood levels are not a problem. Fruits and vegetables are your best source of potassium.

Chapter Six
Herbals and Other Natural Products

Herbal supplements

When faced with kidney disease you may feel frustrated with your inability to cure your disease. You may feel further frustration by the numerous medications that your physicians prescribe for you. Feeling a lack of control and/or fear in your care may cause you to want to try alternative treatments such as herbal remedies or vitamin supplements to treat your disease "naturally." Though some may be of help, several of these treatments need to be used cautiously.

The herbal supplement manufacturing process is poorly controlled, with 70%of the herbals not containing the ingredients stated on the label, and an estimated 20% containing toxic chemicals. In kidney disease this could lead to complications in your treatment, and these toxins could worsen your kidney function.

Some herbs are high in potassium, which can also be dangerous. Others can cause an increase in your blood pressure or cause bleeding. Still others may interact with medications prescribed to prevent kidney rejection after receiving a transplant.

Before you use any herbal remedies check with a health care professional who is familiar with these products. Resources for information can be a renal dietitian or pharmacist, and some physicians are quite knowledgeable on herbal remedies and their risks. Some of the more common herbs of concern are:

Chaperrel	Pennyroyal
Comfrey	Snakeroot
Deadly Nightshade	Yohimbe
Foxflove	Diuretics - dandelion
Germander	Laxatives- cascara, senna
Henbane	Licorice root
Kava kava	Mandrake
Lily of the Valley	Ma Huang - ephedrine
Skullcap	Chine herbal preparations
Guar gum	Echinacea
Mistleltoe	

There are other products to be careful of with your medications. It is important to alert your pharmacist, physician and/or dietitian if you are taking or plan to take:

Ginko, Ginseng, Garlic, Valaria, Kava Kava, St.John's Wort, Gingko

The following are good resources for further information on herbal remedies:

American Botanical Council

P. O. Box 1444345

Austin, TX 78714-4345

www.herbalgram.org

Herbal Research Foundation

1007 Pearl St Suite 200

Boulder, CO 80302

303-449-2265

www.herbs.org

United States Pharmacopeia

12601 Twinbrook Parkway

Rockville, MD 20852

301-816-8223

www.usp.org

Other sites for herbal product information:

www.quackwatch.com

www.consumerlab.com

Some herbs are known to be highly allergenic such as ragweed, daisy, aster, and chrysanthemum. Watch out for these herbs if you are a person susceptible to allergies.

Vitamins and Mineral Supplements

You may need a vitamin supplement especially if you are not eating well. However, your selection of an appropriate vitamin supplement is crucial. Several supplements are high in fat-soluble vitamins. When your kidney function is less than 50% these can be dangerous. Your body does not metabolize fat-soluble vitamins like they did before your kidney disease. As a result, they can get stored excessively in your tissues. Blood levels of these vitamins, such as vitamin A and D, have been found to be at toxic levels in kidney disease patients who are supplemented unnecessarily. Work with your physician on finding the best vitamin preparation. Usually a water-soluble vitamin is recommended.

Some recommended brands are:

Nephrovite, Renex, Nephrocap, Dialyvite. The telephone numbers for the companies who make these, along with other vitamin recommendations can be found in the Appendix E.

The only fat soluble vitamin recommend is vitamin E and even with this one you should not take more than 400 IU of mixed tocopherals per day. Individual amounts of vitamin D may be needed depending on measured levels of this vitamin in your blood.

This is one of the reasons a vegetarian diet can be so beneficial in kidney disease. Eating a variety of plant products can give you many of these trace minerals and vitamins in amounts that your body can use safely.

Chapter Seven
Common Problems

SOME COMMON PROBLEMS WITH KIDNEY DISEASE

Thirst

Feeling thirsty is a very common problem with kidney disease. The cause can be due to the waste product or a solute called urea building up in your blood. This solute is giving your body a signal to "dilute" it. In addition, it can be due to a high salt diet, some medications, or if you are diabetic it can be caused by high blood sugars. Being extra thirsty can be a problem if you are receiving dialysis, not urinating regularly, or if you have edema, water retention in the tissues. If you are on dialysis and you drink too much liquid it stays with you until your next dialysis treatment. If you are taking water pills and you take in excess liquid the pills do not work as well. In either case, excess fluid can put pressure on your heart, causing congestive heart failure.

Ways to treat this problem:

- Make sure if you are dialyzing that you receive your full treatment time. If you are constantly late for your treatment or come off early you may be missing vital minutes to "clean" your blood more thoroughly. This means there will be higher levels of urea that will trigger thirst. This thirst may cause you to drink more than can be removed during your treatment.

- If you are diabetic watch your blood sugars. If needed, see your diabetes specialist or a diabetes educator to re-adjust your insulin or oral medication for better control. Often insulin needs changing with kidney failure.

- Check the salt in your diet. Overall a vegetarian diet is low in sodium, but if you are using a lot of meat analogues, you may be getting more than your recommended sodium allowance for the day. If you are using a meat analogue that has more than 700 mg of sodium per serving you may want to find another product. Appendix E lists several product information sheets where you may find some of these foods.

- Review your medications with a qualified pharmacist. The pharmacist can tell you which medications are making you thirsty. One example is Benadryl or other antihistamines. Discuss the medication with your physician to see if you can be switched to other brands or maybe discontinue them all together

Taste

Many people with kidney disease complain of changes in taste for foods. This is particularly true when your kidney function is down to about 25-30% function. This is due to urea build up in your blood and often improves with regular dialysis. However, this change in taste can also be caused by a zinc deficiency. If you have been eating poorly you may not be receiving enough zinc and may require supplementation. Ask your physician to test your zinc level. However, do not supplement your diet with additional zinc until you find out what your level is running. Supplementing with zinc when you are not deficient can cause other nutrient imbalances in your body.

Nausea or vomiting

It is not uncommon to have bouts of nausea or even vomiting with kidney disease. This is most common right before you require RRT or when your kidney function is around 20% or less. If you are experiencing this problem you may need to supplement your diet with a high calorie and protein drink. There are several on the market and which one you pick will depend on your medical problems. A few of them are:

> ENSURE PLUS, RESOURCE PLUS Moderately high calorie and high protein drink. Needs to be used cautiously when having potassium or phosphorus problems.
>
> GLUCERNA OR RESOURCE DIABETIC Moderately high calorie and high protein drink. Low in carbohydrates and high in fiber. Often used by diabetics, for better blood sugar control. Needs to be used cautiously when having potassium or phosphorus problems.

SUPLENA Often used to give a lot of calories when you have very little kidney function but are not receiving dialysis. This is also very low in protein.

NV RENAL OR NEPRO Very high calorie and protein drink given when receiving dialysis. These are somewhat more expensive than Ensure or Resource. They are often recommended when calories and protein are needed without a lot of potassium and phosphorus.

These products may need to be special ordered by your pharmacy or you can contact the company yourself. See Appendix E for contact numbers.

<u>Constipation</u>

Some of the medications you take for your kidney disease may cause constipation. This can be very frustrating. Making sure you select high fiber foods can help a great deal. Choose fruits and vegetables with skins. Select whole grains, such as brown rice, barley and whole wheat bread, and add in a high fiber cereal, too. See the following list for further suggestions. If you are not used to high fiber cereals, it is always a good idea to gradually add this to your diet. If you do not do this, you could experience additional stomach and digestion discomfort.

FIBER CONTENT OF FOODS
TABLE 10

HIGH FIBER FRUIT

Fresh apple with skin - 1 small
Fresh blackberries - 1/2 cup
Fresh blueberries - 1/2 cup
Fresh sweet cherries - 1/2 cup
Fresh grapefruit - 1/2 small
Fresh grapes - 15
Fresh pear with skin - 1 small
Fresh pineapple - 1/2 cup
Fresh raspberries - 1/2 cup
Fresh strawberries - 1/2
Fresh tangerine - 1 small

HIGH FIBER VEGETABLES

Raw cabbage - 1/2 cup
Raw carrot - 1 small
Raw celery Stalk - 1
Fresh cucumber - 1/2 cup
Raw sweet green pepper - 1/2 cup
Lettuce. all kinds - 1 cup
Radish - 1/2 cup
Raw zucchini - 1/2 cup

HIGH FIBER CEREALS

Ralston Wheat Chex - 3/4 cup
General Mills Wheaties - 3/4 cup
Shredded Wheat - 1 biscuit
Quaker Oats - 1/2 cup, cooked or 1
packet Instant
Ralston - 1/2 cup, cooked
Wheatena - 1/2 cup, cooked
Brown rice - 1/2 cup, cooked

SNACK

Unsalted Popcorn - 1-1/2 cups

Fiber supplements can also be used to aid in the treatment of constipation. These are tasteless and can be easily added to your food. Some of these supplements are Unifiber or Benefiber. Information on how to buy these supplements can be found in Appendix E.

<u>Diarrhea</u>

There can be several reasons for diarrhea with kidney disease. Most often it is due to medications or infections. If you are diabetic your diabetes can also cause this problem. Some of the following ideas may help you. However, if the problem persists even after trying these things, make sure and discuss this with your physician. Prolonged diarrhea can lead to poor absorption of nutrients, which will further compromise your health.

Sometimes milk products can cause diarrhea. Milk products are high in a sugar called lactose that some people do not tolerate well. If you think you are lactose intolerant try eliminating all milk, cheese, pudding, yogurt, foods with dry milk powder in them and see if this helps your symptoms.

Sometimes use of sugar substitute products such as sugar-free candy, puddings, gelatin, cookies or beverages can cause stomach upset and diarrhea. These foods contains a sugar alcohol such as mannitol, sorbitol, or xylitol, that can be hard to digest by some people.

The following foods will help with diarrhea by absorbing water and slowing down digestion, at the same time providing bulk and form to your stool:

- Apple/Pear with the skin-1 small
- Applesauce-1/2 cup
- Oatmeal or Grits-3/4 cup
- White rice-3/4 cup
- Cornflakes-1 cup
- Corn (fresh or canned) -1/2 cup
- Fresh salads (lettuce, green pepper, carrots, cucumbers)-1 cup
- Macaroni or spaghetti -3/4 cup
- Try Congee-1/2 cup rice cooked in 2-3 cups of water- eat small amounts throughout the day

An amino acid called L-Glutamine has showed promising relief to diarrhea problems. L-Glutamine supplements can be purchased at your health food store or from pharmaceutical companies. A dose of 500 mg two times per day is recommended. In the Appendix E are contacts for buying this supplement.

If you have been on a course of antibiotics followed by diarrhea you may benefit from adding acidophilus to your food. This friendly bacterium is often destroyed during antibiotic treatment. Acidophilus helps maintain the normal flora of your digestive tract, which helps with regularity. With antibiotic treatment this friendly bacteria can be destroyed. Make sure when you purchase acidophilus that it is refrigerated, for at room temperature acidophilus is slowly destroyed. It comes in such types as acidophilus bifidus or lactobacillus acidophilus. Fructooligosaccharides (FOS) is a nondigestable carbohydrate that also helps increase this bacteria. Some people find a combination of these works best. This supplement can be found in capsule or powder form. If in powder form it can be blended into food such as hot cereal, juice or applesauce. For best results, try to use these products 2 – 3 times per day.

Itching

Itching is very common in kidney disease and can worsen as your kidney function decreases. There are several reasons for this to occur. This includes too much phosphorus in your blood, uremia or a deficiency in Omega 3 fatty acids. Try the following if you itch:

- Have your phosphorus level checked. If it is high, make sure you are limiting your milk group to the amount allowed. Check the types of beans you are using to make sure they are the lower phosphorus ones. If you are taking "binders" make sure you do not forget to take them. Always take them right before you eat, to get the greatest benefit.

- If you are uremic and on dialysis make sure you are getting your full dialysis treatment time. Even missing five minutes can result in inadequate urea being removed. High blood urea levels can cause itching.

- Try to eat at least 2 sources of omega 3 fatty acids per day. The best source for vegetarians is flaxseed oil (1 tablespoon per day) or flaxseed oil supplements (1000 mg per day). Other source are: soymilk (not low fat or fat free), leafy green vegetables, or walnuts. Greens and nuts need to be considered carefully if you are requiring a potassium-modified diet.

Poor healing

With kidney disease you may find you do not heal quickly. Good nutrition is going to be your best catalyst to heal. If you are not healing well after surgery or from other injuries or trauma, try the following.

- Review your diet. Are you eating all your food groups?
- Weigh yourself. Are you losing weight? If you are, talk to your physician about seeing a dietitian to learn ways to increase your calories. Or add more fat calories to your diet. Again make sure you are eating all the servings in your food groups.
- Take a renal approved vitamin supplement
- Take a supplement of 15 mg of Zinc per day
- Take 300 mg Vitamin C, 2 times per day. However limit this to only a couple months, long-term high vitamin C intake can be dangerous to people with kidney disease.
- If you are still having troubles healing ask your doctor to prescribe a vitamin A ointment. This will often help with healing. DO NOT TAKE VITAMIN A SUPPLEMENTS only topical vitamin A is recommended.
- Try Arginine. Ask your dietitian about Arginine supplements. This is an amino acid found to be beneficial in wound healing. You can get Arginine from the health food store or some pharmaceutical companies. Appendix E has contacts for this supplement. Take 2 times per day for the best results. If the supplement is going to work you will see results

in two weeks.

- If you are diabetic, make sure your blood sugar stays below 120 mg/dl fasting or 140 mg/dl after a meal for good healing.

Restless Legs

Unusual twitching of your legs can often result with kidney disease. This frustrating problem is often resolved by constant moving of the legs. Some of this problem may be due to your kidney disease alone however; certain nutrients can impact the problem such as excess caffeine and alcohol. In addition, deficiencies of carnitine, biotin, or iron can also be factors. Ask to have your carnitine level checked to see if you are deficient. A supplement of L-Carnitine 500 mg per may help if you are deficient. Make sure your renal vitamin has biotin added if not, seek one that does. Make sure you are being checked and treated if you are iron deficient. It is most important that your physician check a Ferritin level. This is often found to be low in Restelsss Legs. Even with a normal hematocrit, hemoglobin or serum iron level, a Ferritin level between 50 and 100 mg/dl is recommended with this disorder. If your Ferritin is less than this, taking oral iron, at least 300 mg per day up to 3 times per day is recommended. Good iron supplements for low Ferritins are polysaccharide iron complexes, such as Niferex. Low Ferritins are common in kidney disease. Other nutrients worth checking for deficiency are folic acid, B-12 and magnesium because these also can contribute to this disorder. If all of these blood tests are normal, medications called dopamine agonists can usually resolve your symptoms. Discuss this with your physician.

WHEN TO SEEK PROFESSIONAL HELP

This book is intended to help you in planning your diet, however, there may be times when you will require the help of a Registered Dietitian who specializes in kidney disease and in addition is supportive of your desire to eat vegetarian. Some signs you may require more help in your diet planning is if

1) You lose more that 10% of your body weight in 3 months

2) You are running a very high potassium and/or phosphorus which you are unable to get into the normal range on your own

3) Your kidney function is below 20%

4) Your albumin, a protein in your blood, is less than 3 g/dl

5) You are very nauseated and having trouble finding things you can eat

Chapter Eight
Recipes and Meal Plans

DAY 1	50 GRAM	60 GRAM	70 GRAM
Breakfast	1 slice toast **margarine** 1 cup oatmeal ½ cup diced peaches 1 cup soy milk	2 slice toast **margarine** 1 cup oatmeal ½ cup diced peaches 1 cup soy milk	2 slice toast **margarine** 1 cup oatmeal ½ cup diced peaches 1 cup soy milk
Lunch	¾ cup tofu eggless salad 2 slices bread lettuce slice **mayonnaise** apple	¾ cup tofu eggless salad 2 slices bread Lettuce slice **mayonnaise** apple	¾ cup tofu eggless salad 1 soy cheese slice Lettuce slice 2 slices bread **mayonnaise** apple
Dinner	¾ cup Tuno casserole* 2 slices bread **margarine** ½ cup green beans 1 cup berries **with non dairy whipped topping**	1 cup Tuno casserole* 2 slices bread **margarine** ½ cup green beans 1 cup berries **with non dairy whipped topping**	1 cup Tuno casserole* 2 slices bread **margarine** ½ cup green beans 1 cup berries **with non dairy whipped topping**
Snack	5-6 gingersnaps Jello	5-6 gingersnaps 1 cup soy pudding	5-6 Gingersnaps 1 cup soy pudding

BOLD foods you can add freely to provide extra calories, especially if you are losing weight or have a poor appetite
*See Recipes

DAY 2	50 GRAM	60 GRAM	70 GRAM
Breakfast	1 English muffin **margarine** 2 tablespoons peanut butter and **jelly** peach slice	1 English muffin **margarine** 2 tablespoons peanut butter and **jelly** peach slice	1 English muffin **margarine** 3 tablespoons peanut butter and **jelly** peach slice
Lunch	1 Gardenburger with 1 oz soy cheese 2 slices bread green salad 1-2 tablespoons salad dressing	1 Gardenburger with 1 oz soy cheese 2 slices bread green salad 1-2 tablespoons salad dressing	1 Gardenburger with 2 oz soy cheese 2 slices bread green salad 1-2 tablespoons salad dressing
Dinner	Indonesian Fried Rice* 1 cup rice 1 slice bread with **margarine** sherbet	Indonesian Fried Rice* 1 cup rice 1 slice bread with **margarine** Tofu Brownie	Indonesian Fried Rice* 1 cup rice 1 slice bread with **margarine** Tofu Brownie
Snack	1 cup berries with **non dairy whipped topping**	1 cup dry cereal 1 cup soy milk	1 cup dry cereal 1 cup soy milk

BOLD foods you can add freely to provide extra calories, especially if you are losing weight or have a poor appetite
*See Recipes

DAY 3	50 GRAM	60 GRAM	70 GRAM
Breakfast	1 cup oatmeal **margarine** ½ cup soymilk 1 cup blueberries	1 cup oatmeal **margarine** ¾ cup soymilk 1 cup blueberries	1 cup oatmeal **margarine** ¾ cup soymilk 1 cup blueberries
Lunch	½ cup Hummus* 1 full piece of pita bread celery and carrots slices 1 – 1 ½ cup sherbet	½ cup Hummus* 1 full piece of pita bread celery and carrots slices 1 cup ice cream	½ cup Hummus* 1 full pierce of pita bread celery and carrots slices 1 cup ice cream
Dinner	3 Tofu Nouguts* ½ cup steamed broccoli ½ cup coleslaw 1 dinner roll **margarine**	4 Tofu Nouguts* ½ cup steamed broccoli ½ cup coleslaw 1 dinner roll **margarine**	6 Tofu Nouguts* ½ cup steamed broccoli ½ cup coleslaw 1 dinner roll **margarine**
Snack	Jello	Jello	1 cup soymilk pudding

BOLD foods you can add freely to provide extra calories, especially if you are losing weight or have a poor appetite
***See Recipes**

DAY 4	50 GRAM	60 GRAM	70 GRAM
Breakfast	2 pancakes made with soy milk fruit sauce **margarine**	2 pancakes made with soy milk fruit sauces **margarine**	2 pancakes made with soy milk fruit sauce **margarine**
Lunch	Large green salad with 2 oz of seitan 2-3 tablespoon salad dressing hard roll with **margarine**	Large green salad with 1 hard boiled egg and 3 oz seitan 2-3 tablespoon salad dressing hard roll with margarine	Large green salad with 1 hard boiled egg and 4 oz seitan 2-3 tablespoon salad dressing hard roll with **margarine**
Dinner	1 serving noodle casserole made with meatless ground meat ½ cup peas 1 dinner roll with **margarine** peach slice	1 serving noodle casserole made with meatless ground meat ½ cup peas 1 dinner roll with **margarine** peach slice	1 serving noodle casserole made with meatless ground meat ½ cup peas 1 dinner roll with **margarine** peach slice
Snack	bagel 2-3 tablespoons cream cheese	bagel 1 ½ oz soy cheese	bagel 2 oz soy cheese

BOLD foods you can add freely to provide extra calories, especially if you are losing weight or have a poor appetite
*See Recipes

DAY 5	50 GRAM	60 GRAM	70 GRAM
Breakfast	2 Corn cakes* with syrup ½ cup applesauce	3 Corn cakes* with syrup 1 egg ½ cup applesauce	3 Corn cakes* with syrup 2 eggs ½ cup applesauce
Lunch	Couscous Taco* Tofu Brownie*	Couscous Taco * Tofu Brownie*	Couscous Taco* Tofu Brownie*
Dinner	Lentil Loaf* 1cup Rice ½ cup peas and carrots 1 dinner roll **margarine** peach slice	Lentil Loaf * 1 cup rice ½ cup peas and carrots 1 dinner roll **margarine** peach slice	Lentil Loaf * with 1 cup rice and ½ cup peas and carrots 1 dinner roll **margarine** peach slice
Snack	1 ½ cup Cornflakes ½ cup soymilk	1 ½ cup Cornflakes ¾ cup soymilk	1 ½ cup Cornflakes 1 cup soymilk

BOLD foods you can add freely to provide extra calories, especially if you are losing weight or have a poor appetite
*See Recipes

DAY 6	50 GRAM	60 GRAM	70 GRAM
Breakfast	Tofu Milk Shake*	Tofu Milk Shake*	Tofu Milk Shake*
Lunch	grilled soy cheese sandwich with 2 oz of soy cheese apple slices carrots slices	grilled soy cheese sandwich with 3 oz of soy cheese apple slices carrots slice	grilled soy cheese sandwich with 3 oz of soy cheese apple slices carrots slices
Dinner	2 egg omelet 2 toast margarine 2 pineapple rings	2 egg omelet 2 toast margarine 2 pineapple rings	3 egg omelet with soy cheese 2 toast margarine 2 pineapple rings
Snack	1 cup sherbet	1 cup sherbet	1 cup ice cream

BOLD foods you can add freely to provide extra calories, especially if you are losing weight or have a poor appetite
*See Recipes

DAY 7	50 GRAM	60 GRAM	70 GRAM
Breakfast	bagel 2 tablespoons margarine 4 oz juice	bagel 2 tablespoons margarine 4 oz juice	bagel 2 tablespoons margarine 4 oz juice
Lunch	Corn soup* 1 slice bread soy cheese apple	Corn soup* 1 slice bread soy cheese apple	Corn soup* 1 slice bread soy cheese apple
Dinner	Rice and Black-Eye Peas* ½ cup canned beets 1 dinner roll and margarine	Rice and Black-Eye Peas* ½ cup canned beets 1 dinner roll and margarine	Rice and Black-Eye Peas* ½ cup canned beets 1 dinner roll and margarine
Snack	1 English muffin 1–2 tablespoon margarine 1 cup berries	1 English muffin 1–2 tablespoon margarine 1 cup berries	1 English muffin 1–2 tablespoon margarine 1 cup berries

BOLD foods you can add freely to provide extra calories, especially if you are losing weight or have a poor appetite
*See Recipes

TOFU

COOKING WITH TOFU

Tofu is a very inexpensive, easy and nutritious way to include quality protein in your diet. Unlike meats, it takes in the flavor of whatever you cook with it. Tofu is very low in phosphorus, potassium and sodium.

THERE ARE 3 TYPES OF TOFU:

FIRM: This is dense, solid and holds well in stir-fry dishes, soups or on the grill. It is highest in protein.

SOFT: This is a good choice for recipes that call for blended tofu. It works well in oriental soups or milkshakes.

SILKEN: This is a creamier type of tofu which works well in blended dishes like cheesecake or lasagna. It mixes well with sour cream to make a higher protein topping.

TIPS FOR USING TOFU:

- Add chunks of firm tofu to your soups or stews in place of meat or with meat.

- Mix crumbled firm tofu into meatloaf.

- Mash tofu with cottage cheese or sour cream and season to make a high protein spread for toast or crackers.

- Make a tofu burger! Mash soft tofu, breadcrumbs, chopped onion and seasonings together and bake or grill.

- Replace all or part of the cream in soups with silken tofu.

- Make missing egg salad with tofu chunks, diced celery, mayonnaise and a dab of mustard (see Recipes)

- Replace powered milk with tofu milk powder in recipes.

- Stir fry cubes of tofu with ginger, oil and a dab of soy sauce, blend into rice or noodles and put in pita bread.

TOFU FINGERS

Makes 3 servings (4oz each)

2 tablespoons tamari or soy sauce

½ cup cornflake crumbs

1 teaspoon seasoning (garlic powder, curry, paprika or other spice)

12 oz firm tofu, cut into ¼ inch slices vegetable oil for coating the baking sheet

Pour the tarmari into a small bowl. In another small bowl, mix together the cornflake crumbs and seasoning. Dip the tofu into the tamari, then into the seasonings. Place the tofu slices on a baking sheet, lightly wiped or sprayed with oil. Bake at 350 degrees F for 20 minutes, flipping once to brown both sides, or fry the coated tofu in a little oil until both sides are browned.

Per Serving:

Calories	180
Protein	22 g
Total Fat	10 g
Total Carbohydrates	7 g
Sodium	900 mg
Potassium	200 mg
Phosphorus	130 mg

EGGLESS EGG SALAD

Makes (½ cup) 3 servings

1-12.3 oz. package of firm tofu, drained

1 teaspoon each apple cider vinegar & honey

2-teaspoon mustard

½ teaspoon tumeric

2 tablespoons each diced celery & onion

1-teaspoon parsley, chopped

Dash of paprika and pepper to taste

Crumble tofu into a small bowl. In a separate bowl, combine vinegar, mustard, honey and tumeric. Mix thoroughly and pour over crumbled tofu. Add celery, onion, parsley, paprika and pepper. Mix thoroughly. Refrigerate approx. 30 min. to allow flavors to meld.

Per Serving:

Calories	60
Protein	7 g
Total Fat	30 g
Total Carbohydrates	39 g
Sodium	100 mg
Potassium	350 mg
Phosphorus	110 mg

TOFU BREAKFAST SHAKE

Makes 1 serving

3 ounces of firm or regular tofu

1/3-cup whole soymilk or rice milk

1-teaspoon vanilla

½ cup fruit (i.e. strawberries or other low potassium fruit is best)*

OR TRY 2 tablespoons Tang

one or two ice cubes

*banana is pretty yummy but count as your one high potassium food for the day

Blend

Per Serving:
<u>With soy milk and strawberries</u>

Calories	144
Protein	8 g
Total Fat	8 g
Total Carbohydrate	10 g
Sodium	<50 mg
Potassium	200 mg
Phosphorus	120 mg

DESSERTS

TOFU BROWNIE

Makes 12 servings

1-1/3 cups cake flour or unbleached all purpose flour

¾ teaspoon baking soda

½ teaspoon cinnamon

1-12.3 oz. pkg. silken lite tofu (Ex-firm)

¼ cup unsweetened applesauce

1-teaspoon canola oil

¾ cup granulated sugar

1-teaspoon pure vanilla extract

1/3 cup cocoa powder

2 tablespoons walnuts, finely chopped for garnish (optional increases the fat content per serving)

Grease bottom/sides of 8x8" pan with vegetable shortening. Place wax paper on greased pan bottom and grease top of paper. In food processor, blend dry ingredients. Empty into small bowl; set aside. Now in the food processor blend wet ingredients (except cocoa) until smooth and sugar is dissolved. Add cocoa; process until smooth. Add dry mixture all that once. Pulse to blend just until all dry ingredients are moistened. Spread evenly into prepared pan. Sprinkle with chopped nuts. Bake in a preheated 450 degree oven for 20 minutes, or until brownies spring back when touched lightly in center. Let cool in pan for 15 min. before turning out on cooling rack. Cool completely.

Per Serving:

WITHOUT NUTS

Calories	120
Protein	4 g
Total Fat	1 g
Total Carbohydrate	25 g
Sodium	25 mg
Potassium	79 mg
Phosphorus	50 mg

WITH NUTS

Calories	128
Protein	4 g
Total Fat	1 g
Total Carbohydrate	26 g
Sodium	25 mg
Potassium	72 mg
Phosphorus	44 mg

SOY MILK PUDDING

Makes 2 servings

½ cup sugar

2 tablespoons cornstarch

1/8-teaspoon salt

1½-cup whole soymilk

1-teaspoon vanilla

In a saucepan, stir together the sugar, cornstarch and salt. Slowly add the soymilk, stirring to prevent lumps from forming. Bring the mixture to a boil. Lower to simmer, stirring constantly for about 5 minutes, until mixture is creamy and thick. Remove the pan from heat, stir in vanilla and pour into dessert cups. Chill until mixtures sets.

Per Serving:

Calories	300
Protein	5 g
Total Fat	4 g
Total Carbohydrate	75 g
Sodium	75 mg
Potassium	100 mg
Phosphorus	60 mg

BEANS AND LEGUMES:

RICE AND BLACK-EYE PEAS

Make 2 servings

Ingredients:

1-cup rice, raw

2/3 cup frozen black-eye peas

¼ cup chopped onion

1-tablespoon oil

1-tablespoon Morga's Vegetable Bouillon, no added salt

Place the rice and 2 cups of water into a saucepan. Add oil and bouillon. On high heat, bring to a rapid boil. When most of the water has boiled down (in about 5-7 minutes) turn to the lowest heat possible. Meanwhile stir fry onion in oil until translucent. Rinse the beans in fresh water then add onion and peas to the pot of rice, stirring thoroughly. Place a tight fitting cover on the pan and let simmer for 15-20 minutes.

Per Serving:

Calories	300
Protein	10 g
Total Fat	15 g
Total Carbohydrate	95 g
Sodium	10 mg
Potassium	320 mg
Phosphorus	480 mg

HUMMUS

Makes 4 servings

2 cups cooked garbanzo beans

¼ cup bean stock

¼ cup lemon juice

2 cloves garlic

½ tablespoon soy sauce

3 tablespoons tahini

2 tablespoons parsley, chopped

Puree all of the ingredients together and let them sit for at least 30 minutes before eating to let the flavors develop.

Per Serving:

Calories:	106
Protein	4 g
Total Fat	4 g
Total Carbohydrate	14 g
Sodium	135 mg
Potassium	250 mg
Phosphorus	200 mg

CHICK PEA SALAD

Makes 1 serving

½ cup canned chickpeas

1 cup shredded lettuce

¼ cup shredded carrot

3-4 slices of red/yellow bell peppers

¼ cup no added salt canned mushrooms

2 cherry tomatoes

1 tablespoon chopped onion

2 hard-boiled eggs sliced

Place the shredded lettuce on a place and layer with the sliced bell peppers, chickpeas, mushrooms and onion. Top with the sliced boiled eggs.

Per Serving:

Calories	300
Protein	21g
Total Fat	12 g
Total Carbohydrate	40 g
Sodium	165 mg
Potassium	900 mg
Phosphorus	395 mg

LENTIL LOAF

Makes 4 servings

1 small onion, chopped

1 tsp olive oil

2 cups cooked lentils, drained

½ cup breadcrumbs

1 cup rolled oats

½ teaspoon thyme

½ cup tomato puree

1-tablespoon vinegar

½ teaspoon salt

Sauté the onion in the olive oil until soft. Preheat the oven to 350. Add the sauteed onions to the remaining ingredients, and mix well. Press the mixture into a loaf pan, cover with aluminum foil or a cookie sheet, and bake for 20 minutes. Uncover and bake for 10 minutes more.

Per Serving:

Calories	280
Protein	14 g
Total Fat	3 g
Total Carbohydrate	50 g
Sodium	300 mg
Potassium	580 mg
Phosphorus	300 mg

MEAT ANALOGUES

INDONESIAN FRIED RICE

Makes 8 servings

Cook until tender according to the following directions:

2 cups of brown rice in 4 cups water

This method of cooking insures that each grain will be separate and the rice will have a delicious nutty flavor. For every cup of brown rice use 2 cups liquid. Heat a 2-quart pan and add the rice. Cook and stir over medium heat for 6-8 minutes, or until rice begins to pop. Remove from heat, add the hot water or vegetable stock, being careful of steam. Cover pan, return to heat, reduce heat to low and simmer 30-40 minutes until rice is tender and liquid is absorbed.

Turn out on a large platter to cool.

Mix and set aside:

1-cup meatless ground meat

1-tablespoon ketchup

1-tablespoon tamari

Microwave approximately 2 minutes to heat through.

Have ready:

1 onion, sliced in half moons 1 red pepper, cut in inch squares

1 carrot, cut in thin match sticks 1-cup celery, diced

1 green pepper cut in inch squares

Heat a wok or large skillet and add:

2-tablespoon dark sesame oil

2 cloves garlic, minced

1-tablespoon gingerroot, minced

Add the vegetables and stir-fry over medium high heat about 5 to 8 minutes. Add the meatless ground meat crumble in the cooled rice. Stir to mix and heat through, adding: 2 Tbsp. tamari

Taste and add a little salt if needed or more soy sauce. Serve hot, topped with sliced green onions.

Per Serving:

Calories	200
Protein	10 g
Total Fat	5 g
Total Carbohydrate	33 g
Sodium	175 mg
Potassium	425 mg
Phosphorus	190 mg

TUNO NOODLE CASSEROLE

Makes 10 servings

1 12-ounce package egg noodles

4 stalks celery, chopped

¼ cup chopped green pepper

¼ cup chopped red pepper

1 10-3/4 ounce can cream of mushroom soup

1-cup low-fat milk (2%)

1-cup sour cream

1 12-ounce cans Worthington Tuno, drained (use ¾ of a can for a milder flavor)

Topping:

1 cup bread crumbs (cornbread also works well)

2 tablespoons grated Parmesan cheese

In a large kettle, cook noodles according to package directions. Drain. Pour noodles into large bowl and add all other ingredients – except breadcrumbs and Parmesan. Stir well. Pour into 9" x 13" baking pan.

In a small bowl, mix breadcrumbs and Parmesan cheese. Sprinkle over noodle mixture. Bake in 350 oven for 35 to 40 minutes.

*If you like the taste of fish, you will love this recipe. The combination of flavors is wonderful, **and the preparation is so easy!***

<u>Per Serving:</u>

Calories	300
Protein	12 g
Total Fat	11 g
Sodium	450 mg
Total Carbohydrates	39 g
Potassium	360 mg
Phosphorus	200 mg

GRAINS AND VEGETABLES

COUSCOUS TACOS

Makes 8 Servings(tacos)

1-cup quick cooking couscous

1-½ cups boiling water

2 teaspoons extra virgin olive oil

½ ripe avocado, peeled and cut into chunks

½ medium tomato seeded and diced small

½ cup chopped red onion

8 corn tortillas

1 cup shredded cheddar cheese or soy cheese equivalent

2 cups shredded iceberg lettuce

In medium bowl, combine couscous, boiling water and olive oil. Mix, cover and let sit for 5 minutes. Remove cover and fluff with fork.

In another medium bowl, coarsely mash avocado.. Stir in tomato and onions. (You can also add any or all of the following: a little lemon juice, hot sauce, chopped cilantro, salt, pepper)

Heat tortillas in the oven.

To assemble taco, spread warm tortillas with avocado mixture. Top with couscous, cheese and lettuce. Fold in half and enjoy.

Per Serving:

Calories	250
Protein	9 g
Total Fat	10 g
Total Carbohydrates	31 g
Sodium	175 mg
Potassium	391mg
Phosphorus	190 mg

FRESH CORN CAKES

Makes 12-3 inch cakes

3 large ears fresh corn

1 large egg, or vegan equivalent **

¼ cup unbleached white flour

½ teaspoon baking powder

Salt and pepper, to taste

Cooking spray or oil

1. With a small, sharp knife, cut kernels from cobs (you should have about 2 cups).

2. In a food processor, pulse corn until chopped. Add remaining ingredients and process until smooth. Let batter sit for 5 to 20 minutes. Stir batter before frying cakes.

3. Lightly spray or oil a large nonstick skillet or griddle. Cook heaping tablespoons of batter over medium-high heat until beginning to brown around the edges, about 2 minutes. Flip and finish cooking, about 1

Per Serving:

Calories	37
Protein	2 g
Total Fat	1 g
Total Carbohydrate	10 g
Sodium	27 mg
Potassium	83 mg
Phosphorus	25 mg

** <u>Egg replacements</u>: Eggs can be replaced by other ingredients in many different ways. 2 oz of mashed tofu works in most casseroles, pancake mixes, lentil loafs or the corn cake recipe above. 2 tablespoons of a thick liquid such as thin applesauce or soy yogurt can also be used. In addition, commercial egg substitutes are available in most health food stores and food co-ops.

SEITAN

HOMEMADE SEITAN

7 ½ cups whole wheat unenriched flour

6 cup water

Pour flour into a large bowl and slowly stir in 6 cups of water. Keep

stirring until the mixture forms a ball. Knead for 10 minutes to develop the

gluten in the wheat. Remove the ball from the bowl and hold it under cold

running water, stretching the dough repeatedly until the starch and bran

wash away, about 10 minutes. Form the dough into a loaf, and place it on

cheesecloth and tie the ends. Then set it in a pot of boiling vegetable stock

flavored to your liking and simmer 1 hour. Add more boiling water to the

pot as necessary. Remove the loaf and let it cool. Slice it or cube it and

use it in recipes where you want a meaty texture and flavor, such as soups,

salads or casseroles.

Per Serving:

Calories	3400
Protein	100 g
Total Fat	8 g
Total Carbohydrate	712 mg
Sodium	25 mg
Potassium	900 mg
Phosphorus	825 mg

FAJITAS

Serves 4

4 - Whole Wheat fajita wrappers, wrapped in foil

1 small red onion, copped

2 medium cloves garlic minced

2 bell peppers, seeded and sliced into strips

1 pound of seitan, cut into thin shreds

1 tablespoon chili powder

1 tablespoon soy sauce or tarmari

2 plum tomatoes peeled and finely diced

low fat sour cream

Place the fajita wrappers in a 200 F ^{0} oven to heat while you prepare the filling. Spray a medium skillet with olives oil cooking spray, add the onion and cook, stirring, over medium heat-low heat until softened slightly. Add the minced garlic and bell peppers and cook, stirring frequently, 5 minutes more. Add the seitan, chili powder and soy sauce or tamari. Lower the heat And simmer 5 minutes.

Place the fajita wrappers under a napkins to keep them warm and arrange the fajita filling on a small platter. Spoon a small amount of sour cream and tomato for garnish.

Per Serving:

Calories	325
Protein	30 g
Total Fat	4 g
Total Carbohydrate	35 g
Sodium	675 mg
Potassium	250 mg
Phosphorus	80 mg

APPENDICES

APPENDIX A

BLOOD VALUES THAT ARE MONITORED WITH KIDNEY DISEASE:

Discussed below are the blood tests commonly monitored in kidney disease. By understanding these blood tests you are better able to manage your diet and in turn your health.

Lab test *Normal*

Potassium 3.5 - 5.5 mmol/L

Reasons for Abnormal Values

If HIGH:

- Eating too many fruits, vegetables, and juices
- Dialysis solution may be too high in potassium if on hemodialysis
- Weight loss or internal bleeding
- Very high blood sugar

If LOW:

- Not eating well
- Vomiting or diarrhea
- Dialysis solution may be too low in potassium

Lab test Normal

Albumin 3.5 - 5.5 g/dL

Reasons for Abnormal Values

If LOW:

- Not eating enough protein
- Calorie intake too low
- Protein loss in urine
- Inflammation process i.e. sickness, infection, etc.

Lab Test *Normal*

BUN less than 100 mg/dL (if on dialysis)

(blood urea

nitrogen)

Reasons for Abnormal Values

If HIGH (> 100 and on dialysis):

- Not dialyzing long enough
- Protein intake too high

NOTE: *If you are not on dialysis, your BUN will also be high. But your physician will determine what it means to you.*

Lab Test *Normal*

Phosphorus 2.5 - 5.5 mg/dL

Reasons for Abnormal Values

If HIGH:

- Not taking enough binders
- Not taking binders at the right time
- Eating too many dairy products

If LOW:

- Taking too many binders
- Not eating well
- Vomiting or diarrhea

Lab Test *Normal*

Calcium 8.5 - 11.0 mg/dL

Reasons for Abnormal Values

If HIGH:

- Taking too much calcium supplement or Vitamin D

If LOW:

- Not taking enough calcium supplement or Vitamin D

Lab Test *Normal*

Alkaline

Phosphatase 38-110 U/L

Reasons for Abnormal Values

If HIGH:
- Poor calcium and phosphorus balance
- Possible kidney bone disease

Lab Test *Normal*

Cholesterol 150 - 200 mg/dL

Reasons for Abnormal Values

If HIGH:
- Eating too many fatty foods
- Eating too many saturated fatty foods
- Not eating enough fiber food
- Above ideal body weight

If LOW:
- Not eating enough

Lab test *Normal*

Hematocrit greater than 36%

Reasons for Abnormal Values

If HIGH:

- Too many red cells
- Dehydration

If LOW:

- Blood loss
- Low iron stores
- Need erythropoietin or more erythropoietin

If LOW:

- Excess fluid
- Certain kidney disease

Lab Test Normal

Creatinine .5-1.7 mg/dL

Reasons for Abnormal Values

If HIGH:

- Not enough dialysis
- Decreasing kidney function
- More muscle mass

If LOW:

- Low body mass

APPENDIX B

MEDICATIONS AND DIET

With kidney disease you may require several medications. Some of these medications can be influenced by the foods you eat. Some of the more common food that interact with you medications are as follows:

MEDICATION	PURPOSE	FOOD INTERACTION
Fosinopril Sodium-Monopril Lisinopril –Prinivil, Zestril	Blood Pressure	Natural Licorice
Paraxetine –Paxil Other SSRI	Anti-depressant	No St Johns Wort, tryptophane supplements
Phenobarbital Dilantin	Anticonvulsant	Avoid >80 mg B6 per day and caffeine, may increase need for folic acid
Omeprazole-Prilosec	Antiulcer	May increase need for vitamin B-12
Prochlorperzine	Antiemetic	Limit caffeine, no alcohol
Propanolol –Inderol Labetolol-Normadyne	Cardiac	Avoid natural licorice, avoid > 2 g vitamin C per day
Feldoipine –Plendil	Blood Pressure	Avoid grapefruit and grapefruit juice 2 hours before or after taking
Furosemide-Lasix	Diuretic	Not with licorice candy
Metoprolol Tartrate-Lopressor, Topral XL	Blood Pressure	Not with natural licorice
Rantidine –Zantac	Anti ulcer	Limit caffeine
Levothyroxine –Synthyoid	Thyroid	Take iron 4 hours separate
Warfarin- Coumadin	Anticoagulant	Consistent vitamin K intake. Caution with > 2 oz onion, limit garlic, ginger, ginko, avacado
Ammlodipine – Norvasc	Blood Pressure	Not with grapefruit or grapefruit juice
Ciprofloxacin	Antibiotic	Avoid milk and yogurt, limit caffeine. Caffeine will increase the effect of the medication
Corticosteriods	Immunosupressant	Avoid St. Johns Wort
Depakote-Valprioc Acid	Anticonvulsant	May require supplementation with carnitine
Digoxin	Antiarrhythmic	Caution with herbs such as ephedra, guarna and ginsing
Pepcid	Antiulcer	Take iron one hour before. Limit caffeine. May increase need for B-12

APPENDIX C

BEANS AND NUTS

	Protein (gm)	Calories	Potassium (mg)	Phosphorus (mg)	Potassium Group
Nuts:					
Butternuts (1 ounce)	7	174	117	127	Low
Black Walnuts (1 ounce)	7	172	156	131	Med
Peanut Butter, creamy (1 ½ T)	6	140	156	75	Med
Almonds, dried (1 ounce)	6	167	156	148	Med
Dried Beans:					
Winged beans-b (1/3 cup)	6	84	156	88	Med
Chick Peas-b (1/3 c)	5	90	156	92	Med
Lupin-b (1/2 cup)	13	100	200	106	Med
Yellow beans-b (1/3 cup)	5	85	200	108	Med
Mung beans-b (1/2 c)	7	95	200	140	Med
Black beans-b (1/3 c)	5	75	200	80	Med
Black Eye-f (1/3 c)	5	75	200	70	Med
*Humus (1/2 c)	6	210	200	137	Med
Lentils-b (1/3 c)	6	77	237	119	Med
Soy beans, green-b (1/2 c)	12	64	470	140	High
Red kidney beans-b (1/3 c)	5	75	235	84	Med
Soybeans, mature-b (1/2 c)	14	75	470	200	High
Broadbeans-b (1/2 cup)	6	93	235	106	Med
Adzuki –b (1/3 c)	5	70	370	115	High
Navy bean (1/2 c)	7	130	330	140	High
White beans small(b) (1/2 c)	8	130	414	150	High
Pinto beans (1/3 c)	3	45	180	28	Med

*Foods over 200 milligrams of sodium. c=canned, b=boiled, f=frozen N=not significant

One-ounce portion of meat has about 100 mg potassium and 65 mg phosphorus, while 1/3-1/2 cup of beans or an ounce of nuts ranges from 150-300 mg of potassium and 80-150 mg of phosphorus. This is indeed a significant difference, yet careful adjustments in a patient's fruit, vegetable and starch servings will enable the incorporation of these foods into the daily diet plan.

APPENDIX D

TRACKING YOUR PROGRESS:

DATE:								
LABS:								
BUN								
Creatinine								
Chloride								
K+								
P04								
Glucose								
A1C								
WEIGHT								
BLOOD PRESSURE								
DIET:								
Milk								
Vegetables								
Fruit								
Grains								
Protein								
Fat								
Exercise								
Relaxation Technique								

APPENDIX E

PRODUCT INFORMATION:

CALORIE AND PROTEIN SUPPLEMENTS

ENSURE, NEPRO, GLUCERNA, SUPLANA, PROMOD

ABBOTT LABORATORIES

Columbus, Ohio 43215-1724

1-800-544-7595

Also available at many grocery and drug stores

RESOURCE, NV RENAL, GLUTASOLV, ARGININE

NORVATIS

Minneapolis, MN 55440-0370

1-800-333-3785

FIBER SUPPLEMENTS

UNIFIBER

1-800-677-3355

Niche Pharmaceuticals

Roanoke, TX 76262

BENEFIBER

NORVATIS

Minneapolis, MN 55440-0370

1-800-333-3785

MEAT ANALOGUES

Food (Serving size on package)	Protein (gm)	Calories	Potassium (mg)	Phosphorus (mg)	Sodium (mg)	Meat †Servings
Green Giant *Harvest Burgers-F	18	140	430	150	370	2
Morning Star Farms Grillers-F	14	140	117	111	260	2
Quarter Prime-F	24	140	195	206	370	3
Worthington *Tuno-C	6	80	<40	88	290	1
*Vegetarian Burger-C	9	60	<40	56	270	1
Diced Chik-C	7	40	101	49	270	1
*Protose-C	13	130	51	83	280	1
Sliced Chik-C	14	70	172	113	430	2
Veelets-F	14	180	117	104	390	2
*Vegetable Skallops-C	15	90	<40	60	410	2
*Vegetable Steaks-C	15	80	<40	43	300	2
Loma Linda *Big Franks-C	10	110	51	74	240	1
*Linketts-C	7	70	<40	43	160	1
*Little Links-C	8	90	<40	49	230	1
*Redi-Burger-C	18	120	140	140	450	2
*Veg-Burger-C	11	70	<40	58	115	1
Nature Touch *Vegan Sausage Crumbles-F	10	60	78	85	300	1
Kraft *Boca Vegan Burger	16	159	429	N/A	295	2
Yves Tofu Hotdog	9	57	57	N/A	360	1

*Vegan Products: C=canned products, F=products found in the freezer/refrigerator section

†Each serving is approximately 7 grams of protein, which equals one protein serving in your meal plan

Adapted from Anika Avery Grant, Meatless Eating on Dialysis

VITAMIN SUPPLEMENT RESOURCE LIST

Nutrient	RDA or estimated safe & adequate intake	Nephrocaps	NephroVite Rx	Dialyvite 800	Dialyvite 800 with Zinc	DialTx
Vitamin C	50 - 100 mg	100	60	60	60	60
Pyridoxine (B-6)	10 - 50 mg	10	10	10	10	50
Folic Acid	0.8 - 1.0 mg	1	1	0.8	0.8	5
Cobalamin (B12)	6 mcg	6	6	6	6	1000
Thiamine (B1)	1.5 mg (30 - 40 mg in PD pts)	1.5	1.5	1.5	1.5	1.5
Riboflavin (B2)	1.7 mg	1.7	1.7	1.7	1.7	1.7
Niacin (B3)	20 mg	20	20	20	20	20
Pantothenic Acid	10 mg	5	10	10	10	10
Biotin	0.3 mg	0.15	0.3	0.3	0.3	0.3
Calcium	variable, at least 1200 mg	0	0	0	0	0
Vit A (not routinely supplemented in HD but may be needed in PD)	1000 mg RE / 5000 IU	0	0	0	0	0
Vit E	15 IU (up to 400)	0	0	0	0	0
Zinc	15 mg	0	0	0	50	0
Selenium	70 mcg	0	0	0	0	0
Chromium	50 - 200 mcg	0	0	0	0	0
Cost / Purchasing / Ordering Information		Check your local pharmacy	Check your local pharmacy	Hillstead Pharmaceuticals, 1-800-535-7742	Hillstead Pharmaceuticals, 1-800-535-7742	

VITAMN SUPPLEMENT RESOURCE LIST

Nutrient	RDA or estimated safe & adequate intake	RENAX	Biotin Forte	5000 Biotin Forte	Sundown B-complex
Vitamin C	50 - 100 mg	50	200	200	0
Pyridoxine (B-6)	10 - 50 mg	15	25	25	2
Folic Acid	0.8 - 1.0 mg	2.5	0.8	0.8	0.4
Cobalamin (B12)	6 mcg	12	10	10	6
Thiamine (B1)	1.5 mg (30 - 40 mg in PD pts)	3	10	10	1.5
Riboflavin (B2)	1.7 mg	2	10	10	1.7
Niacin (B3)	20 mg	20	40	40	20
Pantothenic Acid	10 mg	10	10	20	0
Biotin	0.3 mg	0.3	0.3	0.5	0
Calcium	variable, at least 1200 mg	0	0	0	35
Vit A (not routinely supplemented in HD but may be needed in PD)	1000 mg RE / 5000 IU	0	0	0	0
Vit E	15 IU (up to 400)	35	0	0	0
Zinc	15 mg	20	30	0	0
Selenium	70 mcg	70	0	0	0
Chromium	50 - 200 mcg	200	0	0	0
Cost / Purchasing / Ordering Information		Vitaline Corporation in Ashland OR. Only available to doctor's & lic. health care practitioners. 1-800-648-4755..	Vitaline Corporation in Ashland OR. Only available to doctor's & lic. health care practitioners. 1-800-648-4755..	Shop Rite NOTE: This vitamin pill is missing several vitamins (Vit C, pantothenic acid and biotin).	

Adapted from work done by Joyce Nelson, RD

APPENDIX F

GLOSSARY

Anemia - A condition where you have a low number of red blood cells in your body. It can make you tired and cold.

Artery - Blood vessels that carry blood from the heart to the tissues.

Artificial Kidney (dialyzer) - A mechanical device which removes waste from the blood and restores chemical balance in the body.

Blood Access - The site that has been surgically established for use during dialysis.

Blood Pressure - The pressure within the arteries. It reaches its peak when the heart beats and drops to its lowest level between beats.

Deciliter - A measure of volume equal to one-tenth of a liter.

Dialysate (bath) - The solution used in dialysis to remove metabolic waste products from the blood.

Dialysis - The process of maintaining the chemical balance of the blood when the kidneys have failed (cleansing the blood).

Dialysis Access - Any device used to connect a person to dialysis. This includes peritoneal catheters, fistulas, synthetic grafts and hemodialysis catheters.

Dry Weight (tissue weight) - A range of normal weight when no excess fluid is present. Your dry weight changes when your "tissue" body weight changes.

Edema - An abnormal accumulation of fluid in body tissues. You can check yourself for edema or swelling on your ankles, hands, face or eyelids.

Erythopoietin (EPO) - A hormone made mainly by the kidneys that tells your bone marrow to make red blood cells.

Fistula - A patient's own vein, that is changed by joining an artery (which has high blood flow), to a vein (which has lower blood flow), causing the vein to enlarge and the vein walls to become strengthened for hemodialysis access.

Graft - A tube or "prosthetic vessel" surgically implanted under the skin and joined to the patient's vascular system for access.

Hematocrit - The percentage of volume of blood that is red blood cells.

Kilogram - A measure of weight. One kilogram equals 2.2 pounds.

Liter - A measure of volume. One liter equals 1.06 quarts.

Milli (m) - A prefix used in the metric system meaning one-thousandth.

Milliliter (ml) - A measure of volume. One milliliter equals one-thousandth of a liter.

Peritoneal Catheter - A soft tube, about 1/4 inch in diameter and 13 -15 inches long, which is inserted into the peritoneal cavity through the skin of the abdomen, providing a small opening into the peritoneal through which dialysis can be placed.

Phosphorus Binder - A medication taken with food that binds with phosphorus so the phosphorus does not get into the blood. The bound phosphorus goes out the body in the stool.

Protein - A nutrient used by the body to replace old or damaged tissues and to build new tissues such as muscle and blood.

Uremia - The accumulation of waste products in the blood that the kidney normally filters into the urine.

Vascular - Refers to the blood vessels and blood carrying system to the body.

Vascular Catheter - A synthetic tube or catheter inserted through the skin into a vessel to access the blood supply for hemodialysis.

Vein - Blood vessels that carry blood from the body tissues to the heart.

Waste Products (Metabolic End Products) - Chemicals produced by normal body functions that are not needed by the body.

METRIC CONVERSION TABLES

98.6 Fahrenheit = 37 Centigrade

1 cc (cubic centimeter) = 1 ml (milliliter)

1 liter = 1000 ml = 1 kg (kilogram)

1 liter = 2 pints = 1 quart

1 kg = 1000 gm (grams) = 2.2 lb. (pounds)

1 gm = 1000 mg (milligrams)

1 lb. = 454 gm

1 kg = 2.2 lb.

1 oz = 30 cc

8 oz = 240 cc = 1 cup

16 oz = 480 cc = 2 cups = 1 pint

1 tablespoon = 1/2 oz = 30 cc

2 tablespoons = 1 oz = 60 cc

FREQUENTLY USED ABBREVIATIONS AND CHEMICAL SYMBOLS

BUN: Blood Urea Nitrogen

Ca: Calcium

cc: cubic centimeter

K: Potassium

kg: kilogram

mg: milligram

Na: Sodium

PO4: Phosphorus

References:

A Clinical Guide to Nutritional Care in ESRD. 2nd Ed. Chicago, IL. American Dietetic Association. 1994

ADA, Vegetarian Practice Group, Fact Sheet: Vegetarian Diet in Renal Disease, 1998

Anderson, J., Blake, J., Turner, J., Smith, B. Effects of soy protein on renal function and proteinuria in patients with Type 2 Diabetes, Amer J Clin Nutr 1998;68(suppl):1347-53S

Anderson, J. Soy Protein Decreases Risk for Heart Disease and Kidney Disease. Health Benefit of Soy Products through the Life Span. Lecture 10/6/2000

Avery-Grant, A. Eating Meatless on Dialysis: A Guide for the Adult Hemodialysis Patient, 1999 (216-229-1100)

Bradley, R. Advance Glycosylated End-Products. Renal Forum. Winter, 5-6, 1997

Brookhyser, J. Cooking with Tofu. AAKP. Renallife, Winter, 1999, p 7

Chamion, EW, Why Unconventional Medicine? New England Journal of Medicine. 1993:328:282-83.

D'Amico, G, Gentile, M.G., Manna, G, et al. Effects of Vegetarian Soy Diet on Hyperlipidemia in Nephrotic Syndrome. The Lancet. 339:1131-1134, 1992

D-Amico, G and Gentile, M. Influence of Diet on Lipid Abnormalities in Human Renal Disease. Amer J Kid Ds.22 (1): 151-157, 1993

Eisenberg, D., et al, Trend in Alternative Medicine Use in the US. 1990-1997. JAMA Nov 11, 1998. 280:1569-1575

Ernst, E. Harmless Herbs? A review of recent literature. The American Journal of Medicine. 1998:104:170-178

Fanti, P. 3rd Annual Symposium Proceeding. Soyfoods in Chronic Renal Disease.1-5, 1999

Fanit, P. Soyfood in Chronic Renal Disease, Third Annual Soyfoods Symposium Proceedings, June 1999 Galup, G. Gallup GH. The Gallup Poll. Public Opinion 1996. Scholerly Resources. Wilmington, DE 1997

Galup, G. and Gallup G.H. The Gallup Poll. Public Opinion 1996. Scholerly Resources. Wilmington, DE 1997

Ginanni, L.and Dreitlein, W.B. Some Popular OTC Herbals Can Interact with Anticoagulant Therapy. US Pharmacist, 1998:80-84

Kopple, JD. Nutritional Management in Kidney Disease. Baltimore, Williams and Wilkens. 1997

Kuhn, M. Herbs, Drugs and the Body. Oldest and Newest Forms of Therapy. Medical Educational Services. Hamburg, NY. 1999

Messina, M. and Messina, V., The Simple Soybean and Your Health. Avery Publishing Group, 1994

Miller, LG. Herbal Medicinals and Selected Clinical Considerations: Focusing on Known or Potential Drug-Herb Interactions. Archive of Internal Medicine, 1998:158

NKF-DOQI, Nutritional Guidelines. New York. National Kidney Foundation, 2000

Pagenkemper, J. Planning a Vegetarian Renal Diet. J Renal Nutr, Vol 5, No 4(Oct), 1995, pp 234-238

Patel, C. Vegetarian Renal Diet and Practical Applications, Renal Nutrition Forum, ADA, Vol 19, No.3, Summer 2000

Pellett, P. Protein Requirements in Humans, Amer J Clin Nutr 1990;51:723-37 92, vol 339: 1131-1134

Pellett, P. Protein Requirements in Humans. Amer J Clin Nutr.51:723-737.1990

Practice Guidelines for Nutritional Care of Renal Patients, 3rd Ed. American Dietetic Associaton, 2000

Richman, A., Witkosdi, J. Herbs by the Numbers. Whole Foods Magazine.1997:20-28

Soroka, N, Silverberg, DS, Greemland, M, et al. Comparison of a Vegetable Based (Soya) and an Animal -Based Low Protein Diet in Pre-dialysis Chornic Renal Failure Patients

Smolinski, S. Dietary Supplement Adverse Reactions and Interactions. Pharmacy Practice News: 1998:20-24

Tyler, VE, Foster, S. Herbs and Phytomedical Products In: Covington TR, American Pharmaceutical Association. 1996:695-713.

Walser, M, Mitch, W, Maroni, B, Kopple, J. Should Protein Intake be Restricted in Pre-Dialysis Patients. Kid Int, 55:771-777, 1999

Yodium M, BenShacher D, Ashkenazi R, al. e. Brain iron and dopamine receptor function. In: Mandel P, De Feudis F, eds. CNS Receptors-from Molecular Pharmacology to Behavior. New Ork: Raven Press;1983:309-321

Young, V. and Pellett P. Plant Proteins in relation to Human Protein and Amino Acid Nutrition, Amer J Clin Nutr 1994, 59(supp):1203S-12S

WEB SITES FOR RECPIES:

The Vegetarian Resource Group: www.vrg.org

Vegetarian Times: www.vegetariantimes.com

Vegies Unite: www.vegweb.com

International Vegetarian Union: www.ivu.org/recipes

Epicurious : www.epicurious.com

Tavolo: www.tavolo.com

Boca Food: www.bocaburger.com

Printed in the United States
217697BV00004B/6/A